Professional development in CALL: a selection of papers

Edited by Christina Nicole Giannikas,
Elis Kakoulli Constantinou,
and Salomi Papadima-Sophocleous

Published by Research-publishing.net, a not-for-profit association
Voillans, France, info@research-publishing.net

© 2019 by Editors (collective work)
© 2019 by Authors (individual work)

Professional development in CALL: a selection of papers
Edited by Christina Nicole Giannikas, Elis Kakoulli Constantinou, and Salomi Papadima-Sophocleous

Publication date: 2019/03/15

Rights: the whole volume is published under the Attribution-NonCommercial-NoDerivatives International (CC BY-NC-ND) licence; **individual articles may have a different licence**. Under the CC BY-NC-ND licence, the volume is freely available online (https://doi.org/10.14705/rpnet.2019.28.9782490057283) for anybody to read, download, copy, and redistribute provided that the author(s), editorial team, and publisher are properly cited. Commercial use and derivative works are, however, not permitted.

Disclaimer: Research-publishing.net does not take any responsibility for the content of the pages written by the authors of this book. The authors have recognised that the work described was not published before, or that it was not under consideration for publication elsewhere. While the information in this book is believed to be true and accurate on the date of its going to press, neither the editorial team nor the publisher can accept any legal responsibility for any errors or omissions. The publisher makes no warranty, expressed or implied, with respect to the material contained herein. While Research-publishing.net is committed to publishing works of integrity, the words are the authors' alone.

Trademark notice: product or corporate names may be trademarks or registered trademarks, and are used only for identification and explanation without intent to infringe.

Copyrighted material: every effort has been made by the editorial team to trace copyright holders and to obtain their permission for the use of copyrighted material in this book. In the event of errors or omissions, please notify the publisher of any corrections that will need to be incorporated in future editions of this book.

Typeset by Research-publishing.net
Cover illustration: © apinan / stock.adobe.com
Cover design: © Raphaël Savina (raphael@savina.net)

ISBN13: 978-2-490057-28-3 (Ebook, PDF, colour)
ISBN13: 978-2-490057-29-0 (Ebook, EPUB, colour)
ISBN13: 978-2-490057-27-6 (Paperback - Print on demand, black and white)
Print on demand technology is a high-quality, innovative and ecological printing method; with which the book is never 'out of stock' or 'out of print'.

British Library Cataloguing-in-Publication Data.
A cataloguing record for this book is available from the British Library.

Legal deposit, UK: British Library.
Legal deposit, France: Bibliothèque Nationale de France - Dépôt légal: mars 2019.

Table of contents

v   Acknowledgements

1   Introduction
Christina Nicole Giannikas, Elis Kakoulli Constantinou, and Salomi Papadima-Sophocleous

11   Attitudes held by teachers when using mobile devices as language aids
Sofia Milagros Waldren

25   Exploring the influence of teachers' education and professional development in Cypriot higher education CALL practices
María Victoria Soulé and Salomi Papadima-Sophocleous

39   Promoting pre-service teachers' inquiry skills in a blended model
Sandra Morales, Sandra Flores, and Claudia Trajtemberg

55   Revisiting the cloud: reintegrating the G Suite for Education in English for Specific Purposes teaching
Elis Kakoulli Constantinou

71   Do EFL teachers transform their teaching with iPads? A TPACK-SAMR approach
Jun-Jie Tseng

87   Personal learning environments and personal learning networks for language teachers' professional development
Cecilia Goria, Angelos Konstantinidis, Bryan Kilvinski, and Betul Eroglu Dogan

101   Assessing the efficacy of VR for foreign language learning using multimodal learning analytics
Tom Gorham, Sam Jubaed, Tannishtha Sanyal, and Emma L. Starr

117   Interpreting technologically fluent classrooms: digital natives' attitudes towards the use of technology in primary schools in Norway
Georgios Neokleous

Table of contents

131 Materials design in CALL: a case study of two teachers of English as creators of digital materials
Ferit Kılıçkaya

145 Enhancing literacy and collaborative skills through blogging: the teenage language learner
Christina Nicole Giannikas

159 How different are European and American foreign language teachers regarding the use of ICT in task-based language learning? Beliefs, attitudes and practices in the classroom
António Lopes

181 #SLA: the impact of study abroad on negotiation of identity on social networking sites
Chika Kitano, Daniel J. Mills, and Megumi Kohyama

197 Author index

Acknowledgements

The editors of *Professional Development in CALL: a selection of papers*, would like to wholeheartedly thank the EuroCALL Association for supporting this publication and the Language Centre of the Cyprus University of Technology, the support of which made the publication of this volume possible.

Christina Nicole Giannikas, Elis Kakoulli Constantinou,
and Salomi Papadima-Sophocleous

Introduction

**Christina Nicole Giannikas[1],
Elis Kakoulli Constantinou[2],
and Salomi Papadima-Sophocleous[3]**

Language teaching instruction has evolved substantially over the past two decades. The changes lie within the evident increase of using new technologies in formal educational settings. Universities, schools, and language institutions across the globe are encouraging educators to use technology tools which will assist in teaching foreign languages effectively. Nonetheless, sufficient Computer Assisted Language Learning (CALL) training is lacking in teacher preparation programmes, even though there is a growing universal interest in technology-proficient language teachers among institutions (Hubbard, 2008). Nichols and Hauck (2011) have identified the insufficiency Hubbard has observed, and refer to it as organisational, theoretical, strategic, and pedagogical training challenges. Teachers are lacking support and training to positively integrate technology into the language classroom. Usun (2009) has found that, although many countries in Europe have official recommendations of technology-related skills for future and practising teachers, the training programmes offered are often general and their organisation and content are decided by individual teacher training institutions.

In-training teachers have the need to clearly learn about the use of technology in the digital age. When applied and integrated appropriately, CALL technologies can support experiential learning and practice in a variety of ways by offering effective feedback to students, enabling collaborative learning, enhancing

---

1. Cyprus University of Technology, Limassol, Cyprus; christina.giannikas@cut.ac.cy

2. Cyprus University of Technology, Limassol, Cyprus; elis.constantinou@cut.ac.cy

3. Cyprus University of Technology, Limassol, Cyprus; salomi.papadima@cut.ac.cy

How to cite: Giannikas, C. N., Kakoulli Constantinou, E., & Papadima-Sophocleous, S. (2019). Introduction. In C. N. Giannikas, E. Kakoulli Constantinou & S. Papadima-Sophocleous (Eds), *Professional development in CALL: a selection of papers* (pp. 1-9). Research-publishing.net. https://doi.org/10.14705/rpnet.2019.28.866

student achievement, encouraging the use of authentic materials, prompting interaction, and motivating language learners (Lee, 2000).

So far, only a small number of publications have been devoted to CALL Teacher Education. Examples include the publication edited by Hubbard and Levy (2006) and the book written by Torsani (2016). The present publication entitled *Professional development in CALL: a selection of papers* comes to give an opportunity to researchers and practitioners to share their professional development in CALL through research and practice.

The purpose of this EuroCALL Teacher Education Special Interest Group (SIG)'s edited volume, supported by the Language Centre of the Cyprus University of Technology, is to respond to the needs of language educators, teacher trainers, and training course designers through relevant research studies that provide technological, pedagogical, and content knowledge. The book focusses on

- professional development in CALL,
- the use of technology in primary, secondary, and tertiary education,
- e-learning facilitators,
- the integration of personal learning environments,
- the use of Mobile Assisted Language Learning (MALL),
- the applications of virtual reality,
- materials design,
- the use of information and communications technology in task-based language learning, and
- the integration of social media networks in language education.

More specifically, in chapter one **Waldren** elaborates on the attitudes of 267 teachers when using mobile devices as language aids. The results of the study demonstrate that participants acknowledge MALL devices as beneficial. However, according to the qualitative results, even though participants recognise the potential MALL devices can provide, most participants did not use them within their classroom. Reasons for this, according to the qualitative data, are the teachers' lack of digital literacy and competency, as well as the potential difficulty of managing classroom disruptions and behaviour when using MALL devices.

In chapter two, **Soulé** and **Papadima-Sophocleous** examine CALL practices in the Cypriot higher education system and their relation to teachers' education in CALL and professional development. The survey study conducted involves 28 second language instructors from public and private universities in the Republic of Cyprus. The survey was designed to assess CALL training, CALL training for technology integration, and CALL practices. The analysis of the data reveals a considerable variety in instructors' training, which ranged from in-service training, seminars, conferences, and lectures on CALL or CALL training as part of Master of Arts or Philosophical Doctorate programmes. The researchers found significant differences in perceptions towards effectiveness of training leading to the creation of computer-based instructional materials. Similarly, differences were found in the frequency of usage of mobile devices, website creators, wikis, and photo-graphic programmes.

In chapter three, **Morales**, **Flores**, and **Trajtemberg** present a case study where they examine the development of reflective inquiry skills amongst pre-service teachers in an English Language Teaching Programme in Chile. The researchers describe a blended model of face-to-face sessions and an online community to foster discussions about classroom related issues. The face-to-face interactions took place in an applied research in teaching English as a foreign language course. Data were collected from a questionnaire, comments on the video enhanced observation platform, and focus groups. Statistical analyses were carried out using R scripts and quantitative content analyses were conducted with Word Clouds. A thematic analysis was performed for the focus groups. The findings suggest that the pre-service teachers' experience in the blended model promoted their understanding of pedagogical issues and their capacity to address them as they embarked on research.

Chapter four presents the work of **Kakoulli Constantinou**. The researcher discusses the second phase of an action research study, which aimed at addressing the problem of lack of appropriate technology tools for the delivery of two blended English for academic purposes courses for first-year students of the Departments of (1) Agricultural Sciences, Biotechnology and Food Science, and (2) Commerce, Finance, and Shipping. The solution suggested involved the integration of the G Suite for Education in the teaching and learning process. The suite was firstly introduced in the academic year 2016-2017, and the feedback obtained then was valuable for its reintegration the following year.

In chapter five, **Tseng** aims to fill a gap in the literature by presenting a study which adopted the Substitution, Augmentation, Modification, and Redefinition (SAMR) model to investigate the degree to which four Taiwanese English as a foreign language teachers enacted their Technological Pedagogical Content Knowledge (TPACK) in the context of teaching English with iPads, as well as identified contextual factors that might influence the levels of their TPACK enactments. Results of the study suggested that, although some of the teachers' iPad-based teaching indicated their competency in transforming their teaching, their teaching was predominantly enhanced by the tablets as a substitute to deliver linguistic input to their students in conventional teacher-centred classrooms. In addition, students access to iPads and a wireless network was considered essential. This technological problem might constrain the teachers from enacting TPACK towards the higher levels of the SAMR scale.

Chapter six presents the work of **Goria**, **Konstantinidis**, **Kilvinski**, and **Dogan**, who discuss their findings on how the pedagogical model implemented in an online postgraduate programme integrates the Personal Learning Environment/ Personal Learning Network (PLE/PLN) concept and practice to support students' learning. Furthermore, the authors elaborate on two case studies from the students of the programme on the integration of the PLE/PLN concept in their own settings as well as its effects on their professional development. The first case study describes how the PLE/PLN concept has become part of the instructional strategy of the teacher and discusses the outcomes of its implementation. The second case study deals with how the PLE/PLN concept has facilitated the professional networking activities of the teacher, and how this has affected the teaching practices.

In chapter seven, **Gorham**, **Jubaed**, **Sanyal**, and **Starr** describe a small-scale pilot study in which participants learned how to write Japanese kanji characters within an immersive virtual reality graffiti simulator (the Kingspray Graffiti Simulator on the Oculus Rift Virtual Reality system). In comparing the experimental group to the non-virtual reality control group in the context of embodied cognition, the authors used a multimodal learning analytics approach: the participants' body movements were recorded using a full-body 3D motion-tracker and clustered with a machine learning algorithm.

Chapter eight by **Neokleous** discusses a qualitative study which provides baseline data on young learner attitudes towards the use of technology in primary schools. The participating students highlighted the importance of the application of technology and acknowledged its potential in the education process. The findings of the study also revealed a general favourable consensus among the interviewees regarding their teachers' efforts to adopt technology in class. Yet, students cautioned that technology-integrated lessons should fulfil specific classroom purposes while stressing at the same time the importance of satisfactory preparation before their implementation.

In chapter nine, **Kılıçkaya** describes the importance of providing pre-service and in-service teachers with sufficient training and practice in integrating technology into their classrooms. The current study aimed to investigate two in-service language teachers' views and experiences on the training which was planned and provided based on their needs and requests. The study benefited from an action research methodology and included two male teachers of English who participated in the study. The participants were exposed to a series of workshops that focussed on creating digital materials using several web-based tools. The findings of the study indicated that, although the participants learned how to utilise the technological tools, the participants' intentions of using the technology, in some cases, were not realised in their classroom practices for various reasons, most of which were directly related to the context of teaching.

Chapter ten presents **Giannikas**'s exploratory research study, which took place in a private language school setting in Greece, and included 52 teenage learners who were introduced to Edublogs for the first time. The aim of the study was to investigate the progress students made in their writing with the integration of blogs in their curriculum, by comparing their blog work to their past in-class and homework writing assignments. The development of the students' collaborative skills was also investigated by evaluating the form and frequency of feedback students gave to their peers.

Chapter eleven presents readers with **Lopes**'s results of a transatlantic survey on technology-mediated Task-Based Language Learning (TBLL). The study was conducted within the scope of the European-funded project PETALL. The aim of the study was to determine the teachers' acquaintance with TBLL and with the potential of information and communications technology for enhancing that approach. The survey also allowed the author to characterise the teaching practices used in the language classroom in terms of this approach. The analysis of the data (by frequency) shows that there is a difference between the US and the EU in relation to TBLL, in terms of familiarity, conceptualisation, and forms of implementation in the classroom. There are also differences in defining the benefits of technology-mediated tasks, as the EU respondents put emphasis on the teacher's creativity and responsiveness to new challenges, whereas the US respondents underlie the importance of it providing communication contexts closer to real life, as well as the opportunity for collaboration and mutual assistance.

The book closes with chapter twelve, where **Kitano**, **Mills**, and **Kohyama** describe an inquiry into how Japanese university students who have participated in study-abroad negotiate their identity on Social Networking Sites (SNSs) when interacting informally in English with non-Japanese interlocutors. SNSs provide a unique opportunity for English language learners to practise their skills in an informal environment and to maintain and develop social connections with non-Japanese partners. Participants expressed that a fear of flaunting their English ability acted as barriers to usage, but the effects of this factor was reduced after their time abroad. Finally, participants found that cultural differences in the usage of SNSs caused some tensions, and forced them to evaluate their own cultural preferences and decide what behaviours to adopt from the target culture.

Professional development in CALL: a selection of papers is a collection of newly-commissioned chapters which unifies theoretical understanding and practical experience. The book aspires to provide an up-to-date picture of content knowledge and execution of CALL training and implementation. The EuroCALL Teacher Education SIG hopes that the present contribution will be viewed as a valuable addition to the literature and a worthy scholarly achievement.

References

Hubbard, P. (2008). Twenty-five years of theory in the *CALICO Journal*. *CALICO Journal*, 25(1), 387-399.

Hubbard, P., & levy, M. (2006). The scope of CAll education. In P. Hubbard & M. levy (Eds), *Teacher education in CALL* (pp. 3-20). John Benjamins.

Lee, K.-w. (2000). English teachers' barriers to the use of computer-assisted language learning. *Internet TESOL Journal*, 6(12). http://iteslj.org/Articles/Lee-CALLbarriers.html

Nichols, G., & Hauck, M. (2011). Teacher education research in CALl and CMC: more in demand than ever. *ReCALL*, 23(3), 187-199. https://doi.org/10.1017/S0958344011000139

Torsani, S. (2016). *CALL teacher education: language teachers and technology integration*. Springer.

Usun, S. (2009). Information and communications technologies (ICT) in teacher education (ITE) programs in the world and Turkey. *Procedia Social and Behavioral Sciences*, *1*, 331-334. https://doi.org/10.1016/j.sbspro.2009.01.062

Introduction

About the editors

Christina Nicole Giannikas (Chief-Editor) holds a PhD in the field of Applied Linguistics. She is a teacher trainer for the Department of Education of the University of Cyprus, an instructor for the Language Centre of Cyprus University of Technology, a freelance TESOL/educational consultant, and a materials writer. Christina's research interests are based in the field of Applied Linguistics, specifically in the areas of CALL, professional development in English language teaching, policies in language education, early language learning, and L2 development. Christina is currently the Chair of the EuroCALL Teacher Education SIG and the Developments Administrator for the IATEFL Learning Technologies SIG.

Elis Kakoulli Constantinou holds an MA in Applied Linguistics, and she is currently a PhD candidate in the area of ESP teacher education. She is an English language instructor at the Cyprus University of Technology Language Centre and a teacher trainer for the Cyprus Ministry of Education and Culture. Her research interests revolve around ESP, ESP teacher education, English language curriculum development, the latest developments in language teaching methods, and the integration of new technologies in language teaching. She is a member of various professional organisations and former Secretary of the EuroCALL Teacher Education SIG.

Salomi Papadima-Sophocleous holds a doctorate in Applied Linguistics. She is the Cyprus University of Technology Language Centre Director, its online MA in CALL Coordinator, and a language teacher trainer for the University of Cyprus Education Department. She is currently an EUROCALL Association Executive Committee member and the Association 9 SIGs' coordinator. Her research interests are in the field of applied linguistics, focussing on CALL, computer assisted language assessment and testing, teacher education, and curriculum development. She is the editor of *The ALCUIN Teacher Guide to Motivating Students to read Literature* (2010), and a co-editor of *CALL Communities and Culture* (2016) and *International Experiences in Language Testing and Assessment* (2013). She is also the author of teaching material:

Geia sou (1995), *Greek! Why not?* (2001), *Voilà 1 & 2* (2002), co-author of *Ça Alors! 1 & 2* (1998, 2002), and the designer and developer of the New English Placement Test Online (NEPTON) (2005). Moreover, she has a special interest in oral history. She is the editor of a series of annual volumes on Limassol oral history since 2007 and the author of *Andreas Papadimas, once a soccer player in Limassol* (2015).

1. Attitudes held by teachers when using mobile devices as language aids

Sofía Milagros Waldren[1]

Abstract

The aim of the study is to establish and understand the attitudes teachers hold when using mobile devices as language aids. Data was collected using a mixed method approach. Both quantitative and qualitative questionnaires were disseminated using 'closed/private' Facebook groups related to Teaching English as a Foreign Language (TEFL) and Teaching English to Speakers of Other Languages (TESOL) to focus the survey on participants that had experience in this field. Approximately 267 participants completed the quantitative questionnaire, whilst only eight participants completed the qualitative questionnaire. The results from the quantitative questionnaire demonstrate that participants acknowledge Mobile Assisted Language Learning (MALL) devices to be beneficial. However, according to the qualitative results, even though participants recognise the potential MALL devices can provide, most participants did not use MALL devices within their classroom. Reasons for this, according to the qualitative data, are due to the teachers' lack of digital literacy and competency, as well as the potential difficulty of managing classroom disruptions and behaviour when using MALL devices.

Keywords: MALL, digital literacy, collaboration, pedagogy.

---

1. Cardiff Metropolitan University, Cardiff, United Kingdom; sofiamariawaldren@gmail.com

How to cite this chapter: Waldren, S. M. (2019). Attitudes held by teachers when using mobile devices as language aids. In C. N. Giannikas, E. Kakoulli Constantinou & S. Papadima-Sophocleous (Eds), *Professional development in CALL: a selection of papers* (pp. 11-24). Research-publishing.net. https://doi.org/10.14705/rpnet.2019.28.867

Chapter 1

1. Introduction

Chartrand (2016) defines mobile devices as small handheld computers that either have a touch display or a small keyboard. MALL therefore refers to the "use of mobile technology in language learning" (Miangah & Nezarat, 2012, p. 309). According to Chartrand (2016), the launch of the first iPod Touch in 2007 marked the beginning of integrating handheld devices into the education market (Apple, 2015). This was the first device that enabled users to listen, watch, and read, all on one device. This was further advanced by the iPad, released in 2010, which saw educators and learners use the same device. Following Apple's success, various education-related software and devices were released, and educational institutions began to show interest in using these devices as language tools (Banister, 2010).

If mobile devices are able to assist students in their language acquisition, then teachers should have developed a range of competences and a range of attitudes towards them. Previous research indicates a positive correlation between students' ability to learn a language and using mobile devices (Begum, 2011; Gromik, 2012). However, the research currently available appears to emphasise how MALL devices are able to aid students in relation to their acquisition of certain language skills (Lu, 2008) rather than address the attitudes held by teachers, or indeed their willingness to deploy them within the classroom. Whilst Ghriebs (2015) has conducted similar research, only seven participants, TEFL university teachers who worked within that university, took part were in this research. In comparison to this research, Ghriebs (2015) uses a very small sample and with all of the participants working within the same university, there is the potential for bias resulting from the participants sharing similar recent experiences.

Aside from the usefulness to the student, there are various other factors that could interfere with teachers' readiness to use mobile devices, such as the digital literacy of the teacher. If teachers lack confidence or knowledge when using MALL devices, then it is unlikely they will use them in their classrooms (Kebritchi, 2010).

Of course it is at the discretion of the teachers and their institutions as to whether they are willing to incorporate MALL devices within their lessons. Therefore, this research addresses the following questions:

- To what degree are teachers' attitudes towards MALL influenced by their digital literacy and their competencies in using MALL?

- In what ways do teachers think MALL is beneficial or detrimental to language learning?

In answering these questions, this research will establish whether teachers perceive MALL devices to be beneficial or detrimental to language learning, and attempt to understand why teachers hold such opinions.

2. Method

This inquiry is interpretivist in nature, where behavioural patterns are observed and assumptions are made about both context and participants based on interpretation of data (Ibrahim, 2014). Interpretivism is suitable for this research as it is based on quantified data regarding the behaviour and attitudes of participants to which the researcher has no direct access and must therefore infer. Interpretivist frameworks explore the attitudes and motives, informed by anonymous qualitative survey data, based on subjective experiences that are linked to context and time (Edirisingha, 2012).

The methodological approach that is best suited for the interpretivist framework is mixed (Ibrahim, 2014), as it can be used to both establish and understand the attitudes the teachers hold towards MALL devices. Mixed methodology refers to collecting, analysing, and integrating both quantitative and qualitative research within a single study (Imran & Yusoff, 2015). The methodology involved in collecting data for this study is referred to as 'mixed methods lite', meaning that the quantitative data was the dominant methodology used (Greene, 2012). The quantitative study was used to describe and define patterns of behaviours and attitudes amongst the participants whilst the qualitative data provides the context necessary to enrich the researcher's understanding of motives behind the behavioural patterns, without necessarily influencing the analysis by hypotheses. The qualitative data in this case provided further understanding of the results, meaning greater insight into inferences, which formulate the findings of the research (Ponce & Pagán-Maldonado, 2015). This research follows the concurrent mixed method design of triangulation in that the qualitative section and the quantitative section are analysed individually and then compared and following that a conclusion is drawn incorporating both data sets (Creswell & Plano Clark, 2007).

In order to collect quantitative and qualitative data, it was decided that the most efficient research instrument would be an online questionnaire, which was created using Google Forms. Considering that the study is an evaluation of attitudes, there was a need to access demographically diverse individuals, with differing experiences. In comparison to face-to-face interviews, or telephone-based interviews, online questionnaires are also able to provide participants with a certain amount of anonymity. This is presumed to accumulate more accurate data, as the researcher is minimising social desirability pressures (Lelkes et al., 2012). Social desirability pressures, in this case, could be teachers feeling incompetent or ashamed by their inability to use MALL devices successfully, particularly as the researcher's aim was to assess confidence.

According to Zhang, Tousignant, and Xu (2012), it is becoming increasingly important for educators to be capable and confident in their digital literacy. If participants are unable or unwilling to use MALL devices, they may feel a certain pressure to conform, which may result in less honest results or simply not participating in the data collection process. Online questionnaires however provide participants with a degree of anonymity, meaning participants are more likely to provide honest answers. It was therefore decided to post the questionnaire as a link within the official TEFL/TESOL Facebook groups, such as *TEFL Teachers in Spain* and *TEFL Org UK*. These were all private/closed groups with members being associated with TEFL/TESOL and were either teachers, students, or recruiters within the field.

Convenience sampling was selected, which is a type of nonprobability or non-random sampling, and participants are those that meet certain practical criteria, in this case their willingness to participate (Etikan, Musa, & Alkassim, 2016), and their membership of the TEFL/TESOL Facebook groups.

The quantitative questionnaire, which participants answered using a Likert scale, collected a total of 267 results from a wide demographic, as demonstrated in Table 1 below.

Table 1. Demographics of quantitative data by age range of participants (N=267)

Age Range	Count	Percentage
<20	2	0.75%
20-35	128	47.92%
35-50	106	39.70%
50-67	30	11.24%
67+	1	0.37%

In regards to the qualitative questionnaire, data was collected from only eight participants. Whilst there is no clear indication as to why fewer participants responded to the qualitative questionnaire (given that both questionnaires were disseminated in the same way and to the same group), it could be explained by the fact that the Likert scale based quantitative questionnaire was less time consuming and easier to complete whereas the qualitative questionnaire provided participants with open-ended questions meaning that answers were not suggested to the respondent, but instead participants were required to answer in their own words; responses were to a degree more descriptive but also more time consuming. The demographics of the qualitative questionnaire are presented in Table 2.

Table 2. Demographics of the Qualitative Data (N=8)

Native English speakers	Non Native English speakers
3	5
Taught in European Union	**Taught outside of European Union**
3	5

Taught in private schools	Taught in public schools
4	4
Full time career as EFL teacher	**Other career**
8	0

In order to complete this study ethically, the researcher followed the guidelines established by the British Educational Research Association (BERA, 2011). Whilst Facebook was used, it was only utilised as a medium to disseminate the questionnaire. Furthermore, prior to respondents completing the questionnaires, a consent form was provided and access to the questionnaire was limited to those who completed it.

3. Results and discussion

3.1. To what degree are teachers' attitudes towards MALL influenced by their digital literacy and their competencies in using MALL?

According to the *Teacher Mobile Learning Adoption Model* (Mac Callum, Jeffrey, & Kinshuk, 2014), one of the main factors, which has been found to directly impact teachers' adoption of technology, is the teachers' ability to use digital technology, i.e. their digital literacy. Digital literacy is measured within the questionnaire by means of assessing the participant's technological ability with regards to mobile software use, with particular focus on language learning. Although all participants must, to some degree, have an understanding of how to use technology, considering the means by which the questionnaire was disseminated, simply accessing social media and completing a questionnaire requires less technological competence compared to that required in deploying MALL effectively in the classroom.

In order to assess teachers' ability to implement MALL devices, participants were given the statement: 'I am confident to use mobile devices for language learning purposes'. Results are displayed in Table 3.

Table 3. Results to teachers' confidence in using MALL devices for language learning purposes (N=267)

Strongly Agree	Agree	Neither Agree nor Disagree	Disagree	Strongly Disagree	No Answer
93	124	33	13	2	2
35%	46%	12%	5%	1%	1%

These results indicate that the majority of the participants (81%) answered positively: agreed (46%) and strongly agreed (35%). This suggests that the majority of participants feel confident enough in their digital literacy that they would be able to use MALL devices successfully within their teaching practices.

However, 12% of participants also stated that they neither agree nor disagree. This could be due to participants not feeling sufficiently competent in their ability to successfully adopt technology, and may require training or support in how to implement such devices successfully, thus achieving digital competency. In order to establish the level of digital competency teachers currently have, the following statement was provided: 'I need training/further training on how to use mobile devices for language learning purposes'. Results are provided in Table 4.

Table 4. Training/more training on how to use MALL devices for language learning purposes (N=267)

Strongly Agree	Agree	Neither Agree nor Disagree	Disagree	Strongly Disagree	No Answer
55	116	59	26	11	0
21%	43%	22%	10%	4%	0%

The results from Table 4 indicate that the majority (64%) of participants agree (43% agree, 21% strongly agree) that they require training. However, as presented in Table 3, the majority of the participants also agreed that they were already confident in their ability to use MALL devices within the classroom. This could indicate that the amount of training teachers receive will not necessarily have a direct effect on the confidence teachers have when using mobile devices as language aids, as it appears that training has only a limited impact on the attitudes that teachers hold. Furthermore, 22% of participants also stated that they neither agree nor disagree to requiring training/more training. This could indicate that, whilst teachers may perceive training to be potentially beneficial, they are unsure whether it will aid in their ability to use MALL devices.

Based on the participants' self-assessment, we can summarise that the majority of participants are digitally literate and confident in their ability to use MALL devices. However, whilst participants claim to be confident in their ability, the majority of participants also state that they require further training in order to be able to use MALL devices successfully. It could, therefore, be interpreted that the amount of training teachers receive does not necessarily have a direct correlation with the confidence level teachers have when using MALL devices, indicating that training has only a limited impact on the attitudes the teachers hold.

3.2. In what ways do teachers think MALL is beneficial or detrimental to language learning?

In establishing the support MALL devices can provide to the students, we can determine their potential net benefits within the classroom. Whether the teachers deem MALL to be a net benefit or a detriment may influence their overall attitudes to it, particularly in a pedagogical sense. One of the benefits MALL devices can provide students with is the ability to enhance learning collaborations. In order to evaluate this, the researcher provided the participants with the following statement: 'mobile devices can increase collaboration between students within the classroom'. Results are presented in Table 5.

Table 5. Devices increase collaboration between students (N=267)

Strongly Agree	Agree	Neither Agree nor Disagree	Disagree	Strongly Disagree	No Answer
63	122	53	25	1	3
24%	46%	20%	9%	0%	1%

Results indicate that the majority of participants (70%) either agreed or strongly agreed that mobile devices are able to increase collaboration between students in the classroom. Increasing collaboration between students has pedagogical benefits, as collaboration can allow the teacher to interact with all students simultaneously with the use of MALL, which may result in more manageable and efficient teaching. However, 20% of participants also indicated that they neither agree nor disagree. Reasons for this could be that the participant lacks experience with MALL devices.

Whilst collaboration is considered a beneficial factor of MALL, research indicates that teachers may find using MALL devices in the classroom to be too distracting for students (Tesch, Coelho, & Drozdenko, 2011). To evaluate whether the participants also perceive MALL devices to be too difficult to manage, the following statement was provided: 'using mobile devices within the classroom for language teaching purposes will be too difficult to discipline and manage'. Results are demonstrated in Table 6.

Table 6. MALL devices being too difficult to discipline and manage (N=267)

Strongly Agree	Agree	Neither Agree nor Disagree	Disagree	Strongly Disagree	No Answer
22	66	81	83	14	1
8%	25%	30%	31%	5%	0%

According to the results displayed, 36% of individuals both disagreed and strongly disagreed, compared to 33% who agreed and strongly agreed. Furthermore, 30% of participants neither agree nor disagree. It appears that these results are inconclusive. Reasons for these inconclusive results could be related to the teachers' specific experience of MALL devices. For example, students playing a game are more likely be more engaged compared to reading or doing other non interactive activities. Therefore, teachers who use MALL devices solely for playing games may have better experiences. Teachers who use MALL devices for other less interactive and engaging activities, may find that students become distracted and do other irrelevant activities. However, due to the nature of MALL devices, it is difficult for a teacher to quantify the amount of work done by the student and this is a potential reason as to why 30% of respondents neither agree nor disagree.

In order to have a better understanding of participants' opinions towards MALL devices as language aids, the following statement was presented: 'in general, I think that mobile devices can be used successfully for language learning purposes and can be useful for students'. Results are presented in Table 7.

Table 7. Results to mobile devices being used successfully as language aids (N=267)

Strongly Agree	Agree	Neither Agree nor Disagree	Disagree	Strongly Disagree	No Answer
123	118	16	7	1	2
46%	44%	6%	3%	0%	1%

These results indicate that the majority of participants strongly agreed (46%) and 44% also agreed to MALL devices successfully enabling language learning, so a 90% positive response. These results indicate that participants perceive MALL devices to be beneficial to students.

3.3. Qualitative data

However, in contradiction to the quantitative section above, according to the qualitative data, when participants were asked: 'what technology do you currently have access to, and what do you expect your students to have access to?', six out of the eight participants indicated that they did not permit their students to use MALL devices within the classroom. According to results from this question, one of the main factors which appears to have influenced teachers' unwillingness to use MALL devices in the classroom is their own digital literacy. Whilst we have suggested within the quantitative results that participants (the teachers) must be digitally literate to some degree, results within this section indicate that participants are not taking sufficient advantage of the potential that MALL devices can provide. One of the participants who did allow MALL devices indicated: "I allow the students to use their mobiles to access dictionaries or look up information" (Participant 5). This indicates that even though this participant understood the potential these devices could provide, they only used them for basic tasks. Reasons for this, according to Participant 8, are: "most of the teachers are not prepared or they don't know how to include the devices in the class planning and activities". This quotation indicates that participants are not sufficiently trained and therefore lack knowledge on how to use MALL devices successfully, which prevents participants from capitalising on their full potential, and explains their unwillingness to use MALL devices. A similar conclusion was also reached by Holden and Rada (2011).

Another barrier, which could also have an effect on why participants are unwilling to use MALL devices, might be the difficulty in maintaining discipline in the classroom when using them. When participants were asked 'do students bring their mobile devices to class?', Participants 4 and 7 state that students are: "not allowed to use them (mobile devices) in the classroom". This issue of management and discipline is another possible indication of why teachers are unwilling to implement MALL devices in the classroom. This is further supported as Participant 4 recognises the potential MALL devices can provide, stating: "if students were allowed to use their mobile devices during class, it would facilitate the implementation of more interactive and meaningful activities in ESL context". This quotation indicates that, even though the strengths of MALL devices are recognised, it appears that either the teachers or their management are still unwilling to implement MALL devices in the classroom. Due to lack of direct access to the participants it is unclear who is prohibiting the teachers from using MALL devices, but we can infer it is likely to be the school management or those responsible for setting education policies.

4. Conclusions

Results from both the quantitative and qualitative data appear to contradict one another. According to the quantitative data, participants indicated that they were confident in their ability to use mobile devices for language learning within the classroom. However, the data from the qualitative questionnaire reveals that participants solely refer to using MALL devices for basic tasks. This could indicate that, even though many teachers believe they are digitally literate, they may still require training to deploy MALL in the class, and/or support for this from the school management/education policy. Although, as presented in the quantitative section, it is not entirely clear whether training has a direct impact on teachers' digital competence level.

However, regardless to how useful MALL devices are in enabling language learning, if there is prohibition emplaced by either the school or the teachers themselves, teachers will be unwilling/ unable to integrate MALL devices into their classroom. The results from the quantitative data indicate that respondents identify that MALL devices are able to assist language learning, as well as enhance student collaboration within the classroom. Participants also indicate concern over the teachers' ability to manage students' behaviour when using MALL devices. Results from the quantitative section appear to be inconclusive in regards to behaviour and management, however, within the qualitative section, two participants stated that students were prohibited from using MALL devices within the classroom. This problem of behavioural management coupled with the inability to use these devices to their full potential could indicate that teachers are simply unwilling or unable to invest the time into using and implementing MALL devices, and instead are left to rely on traditional teaching methods. This could indicate that all the acknowledged benefits of MALL devices, including the pedagogical benefits, are minimised if MALL devices are banned from class by school management, educational policy, or common practice.

References

Apple. (2015). *Ipod + Itunes Timeline*. https://www.apple.com/pr/products/ipodhistory/

Banister, S. (2010). Integrating the Ipod Touch in K–12 education: visions and vices. *Computers In The Schools, 27*(2), 121-131. https://doi.org/10.1080/07380561003801590

Begum, R. (2011). Prospect for cell phones as instructional tools in the EFL classroom: a case study of Jahangirnagar University, Bangladesh. *English Language Teaching, 4*(1), 105-115. https://doi.org/10.5539/elt.v4n1p105

BERA. (2011). *British Educational Research Association.* https://www.bera.ac.uk/wp-content/uploads/2014/02/BERA-Ethical-Guidelines-2011.pdf

Chartrand, R. (2016). *Advantages and disadvantages of using mobile devices in a university language classroom.* https://swsu.ru/sbornik-statey/pdf/gaiken23_1-13.pdf

Creswell, J. W., & Plano Clark, V. L. (2007). *Designing and conducting mixed methods research.* Sage Publications Ltd.

Edirisingha, P. (2012). Interpretivism and positivism (ontological and epistemological perspectives). *Research Paradigms And Approaches.* https://prabash78.wordpress.com/2012/03/14/interpretivism-and-postivism-ontological-and-epistemological-perspectives/

Etikan, I., Musa, S. A., & Alkassim, R. S. (2016). Comparison of convenience sampling and purposive sampling. *American Journal of Theoretical and Applied Statistics, 5*(1), 1-4. https://doi.org/10.11648/j.ajtas.20160501.11

Ghriebs, E. B. (2015). *Teachers' and students' attitudes towards the use of mobile assisted language learning.* http://dspace.univ-biskra.dz:8080/jspui/bitstream/123456789/5807/1/GHRIEB%20EL-Boukhari.pdf

Greene, J. C. (2012). Engaging critical issues in social inquiry by mixing methods. *American Behavioral Scientist, 56*(6), 755-773. https://doi.org/10.1177/0002764211433794

Gromik, N. (2012). Cell phone video recording feature as a language learning tool: a case study. *Computers & Education, 58*(1), 223-230. https://doi.org/10.1016/j.compedu.2011.06.013

Holden, H., & Rada, R. (2011). Understanding the influence of perceived usability and technology self-efficacy on teachers' acceptance. *Journal of Research on Technology in Education, 43*(4), 343-367. https://doi.org/10.1080/15391523.2011.10782576

Ibrahim, R. (2014). *Combining qualitative and quantitative approaches in research.* https://www.linkedin.com/pulse/20141203163542-69677968-combining-qualitative-and-quantitative-approaches-in-research

Imran, A., & Yusoff, R. M. (2015). Empirical validation of qualitative data: a mixed method approach. *International Journal of Economics and Financial Issues, 5*(1S), 389-396.

Kebritchi, M. (2010). Factors affecting teachers' adoption of educational computer games: a case study. *British Journal Of Educational Technology, 41*(2), 256-270. https://doi.org/10.1111/j.1467-8535.2008.00921.x

Lelkes Y., Krosnick, J. A., Marx, D. M., Judd, C. M., & Park, B. (2012). Complete anonymity compromises the accuracy of self-reports. *Journal of Experimental Social Psychology, 48*(6), 1291-1299. https://doi.org/10.1016/j.jesp.2012.07.002

Lu, M. (2008). Effectiveness of vocabulary learning via mobile phone. *Journal of Computer Assisted Learning, 24*(6), 515-525. https://doi.org/10.1111/j.1365-2729.2008.00289.x

Mac Callum, K., Jeffrey, L., & Kinshuk. (2014). Factors impacting teachers' adoption of mobile learning. *Journal Of Information Technology Education: Research, 13,* 141-142. https://doi.org/10.28945/1970

Miangah, T. M., & Nezarat, A. (2012). Mobile-assisted language learning. *International Journal of Distributed and Parallel Systems (IJDPS), 3*(1), 309-319. https://doi.org/10.5121/ijdps.2012.3126

Ponce O. A., & Pagán-Maldonado N. (2015). Mixed methods research in education: capturing the complexity of the profession. *International Journal of Educational Excellence, 1*(1), 111-135. https://doi.org/10.18562/IJEE.2015.0005

Tesch, F., Coelho, D, & Drozdenko, R. (2011). We have met the enemy and he is us: relative potencies of classroom distractions. *Business Education Innovation Journal, 3*(2), 268-277.

Zhang, Z., Tousignant, W., & Xu, S. (2012). Introducing accessible ICT to teacher candidates: a way to address equity issues. *Journal Of Literacy And Technology, 13*(1), 2-18.

2. Exploring the influence of teachers' education and professional development in Cypriot higher education CALL practices

María Victoria Soulé[1] and Salomi Papadima-Sophocleous[2]

Abstract

The present study examines Computer Assisted Language Learning (CALL) practices in the Cypriot Higher Education (HE) system and their relation to teachers' education in CALL and professional development. It involves 28 second language instructors from public and private universities in the Republic of Cyprus. A survey was designed to assess CALL training, CALL training for technology integration, and CALL practices. The analysis of the data reveals a considerable variety in instructors' training, which ranged from in-service training, seminars, conferences, and lectures on CALL or CALL training as part of Master of Arts (MA) or Philosophical Doctorate (PhD) programmes. Despite this variety, the perception of instructors towards the training received for technology integration was generally positive, particularly in terms of its usefulness for the evaluation, selection, and use of computer-based instructional material. However, we found significant differences in their perception towards effectiveness of training, leading to the creation of computer-based instructional materials. Similarly, differences were found in the frequency of usage of mobile devices, website creators, wikis, and photo-graphic programmes.

1. Cyprus University of Technology, Limassol, Cyprus; mariavictoria.soule@cut.ac.cy

2. Cyprus University of Technology, Limassol, Cyprus; salomi.papadima@cut.ac.cy

How to cite this chapter: Soulé, M. V., & Papadima-Sophocleous, S. (2019). Exploring the influence of teachers' education and professional development in Cypriot higher education CALL practices. In C. N. Giannikas, E. Kakoulli Constantinou & S. Papadima-Sophocleous (Eds), *Professional development in CALL: a selection of papers* (pp. 25-37). Research-publishing.net. https://doi.org/10.14705/rpnet.2019.28.868

Chapter 2

Keywords: teacher education in CALL, professional development, CALL practices, Cypriot higher education system.

1. Introduction

There are many factors that can influence teachers' use of computer technology in the classroom (Lin, Huang, & Chen, 2014); teachers' CALL training is a crucial one (Son & Windeatt, 2017). The question of whether L2 teachers' technology training contributes to the integration of computer technology into the classroom has been widely addressed in several studies. For instance, Hong (2010) points out that there is still an insufficient number of quality courses and workshops that integrate technology education into L2 teacher education programmes. Nonetheless, Hong (2010) asserts that many efforts have been made in order to develop and integrate CALL teacher education into L2 teacher education programmes. These efforts include technology workshops, lectures on CALL, online courses, face-to-face courses specifically designed for a CALL certificate, and CALL MAs (Hubbard & Levy, 2006; Reinders, 2009). However, other studies have shown that effective technology integration is not happening, despite training teachers on the use of technology (Ertmer & Ottenbreit-Leftwich, 2010). As Guichon (2009) suggests, this could be explained by the fact that the technologies discovered during CALL education programmes might swiftly become obsolescent after teachers obtain certification.

In addition to recognising the presence of obsolescent technology in CALL education programmes, Kessler (2006) highlights that much of what teachers know about technology for language teaching results from informal or *ad hoc* experience through conference workshops, in-service training, personal reading, and other forms of self-edification. Moreover, in his study, he found that teachers perceive that formal instruction does not serve pedagogical needs, specifically when they need to create their own CALL-based materials. The author emphasises that this is due to the lack of satisfaction with the CALL preparation they received. He also suggests that "formal language teacher preparation programmes have largely neglected to equip their graduates with the related knowledge and skills they need to enter today's technologically advanced language classroom" (Kessler, 2006, p. 23). However, Debski (2006) has demonstrated that an MA in CALL can offer learning opportunities that are adequate in serving the needs of future teachers, not just from a practical perspective but from theoretical frameworks that enable a meaningful integration of technology into teaching and learning.

In the Republic of Cyprus, research on teachers' use of technology and CALL teacher education has been carried out in different educational settings. Vrasidas (2015) conducted a large scale survey in Cypriot public elementary schools, where he found that, despite the rhetoric of reform that dominates education discourse, the adoption of technology was not occurring as expected. The study showed that, although teachers were aware of the benefits of technology integration, the majority were not applying it; this was due to many factors, including inadequate training seminars provided to teachers. Similar results were found in the investigation that Papayianni (2012) undertook in order to determine English language teachers' CALL use in secondary education in Cyprus. According to the findings, in-service teacher training programmes failed to provide teachers with the required technical and pedagogical knowledge and skills to make successful use of technology; that is why, she argues, training is a major factor that influences teachers' decisions in terms of CALL implementation (Papayianni, 2012, p. 126).

In the context of Cypriot HE, previous studies have described the perceptions of second language (L2) instructors towards technology integration in language teaching (Athanasiou & Nicolaou, 2014) as well as the profile of the language centres established in the Republic of Cyprus, and the training provided by these centres to their staff (Papadima-Sophocleous & Parmaxi, 2016). The purpose of the present study is, therefore, to contribute to the description of the current situation of the Cypriot HE system, by examining HE L2 instructors' CALL education and its relation to CALL practices.

2. Method

As a means of better understanding the complexity of HE L2 instructors' integration of technology into the classroom and its relation with CALL education and professional development, the aim of this study was threefold: (1) to determine what kind of CALL education HE L2 instructors in the Republic of Cyprus have received; (2) to examine HE L2 instructors' perceptions towards the CALL training received; and (3) to identify to what extent HE L2 instructors' CALL education and professional development affect their CALL practices.

2.1. Participants

The population of this study consisted of HE L2 instructors from the seven (two public and five private) universities in the Republic of Cyprus. A web-survey was sent out to the 97 instructors employed in these universities. The online survey response rate was 28.8%. It slightly exceeded the return rate of previous research obtained in similar studies that were carried out in different educational contexts (Georgina & Hosford, 2009; Yu, Sun, & Chang, 2010). The majority of language instructors in our sample taught English (50%), followed by Greek (14.3%), Spanish (10.7%), French (7.1%), Italian (7.1%), Turkish (7.1%), and Russian (3.6%). Regarding the instructors' educational qualification, 78.5% were holders of an MA and 21.5% were holders of a PhD. The gender distribution of the instructors was 25% male and 75% female, and their average age was 39.89 (SD 9.5) In terms of their years of teaching experience, their average was 16.14 years (SD 8.02) and their average years of experience as CALL practitioners was 6.82 (SD 2.51).

2.2. Instrumentation and data analysis procedure

The data collection instrument was an online survey. A first version of the survey was piloted in order to context-test the instrument and to obtain some data to be used for item analysis. The final version consisted of four sections. We designed the first section where we included questions targeting the respondent's personal background characteristics. The second section was used to obtain information related to instructors' education, type of CALL training received, and instructors' perceptions towards CALL training usefulness for technology integration. This section included dichotomous questions, multiple choice questions, and a rating scale. The 13 items of this rating scale were adapted from Kessler (2007). The participants were asked to rate their perceptions towards their CALL training based on a five-point Likert scale (1=*completely disagree*, 2=*disagree*, 3=*neutral*, 4=*agree*, 5=*completely agree*). The third section was designed to measure the instructors' frequency of technology use in classroom practices. The 21 items in this section were adapted from Papanastasiou and Angeli (2008). These items were included on a five-point Likert scale (1=*never*, 2=*once per term*, 3=*once per month*, 4=*once per week*, 5=*always*). The last section of four items measured instructors' perceptions towards the technical infrastructure at their working place. A five-point Likert scale ranging from *completely disagree* to *completely agree* was used.

As far as the internal consistency reliability of the instrument is concerned, the sections of the survey that were pertinent to Cronbach's alpha revealed an acceptable value of .899 (Dörnyei, 2010). After the survey had been administered, all responses were recorded and scored for statistical analysis, including descriptive statistics and the Mann-Whitney U test. The Mann-Whitney U test, a nonparametric equivalent of the independent sample *T*-test, was performed to identify if any differences in participants' responses were significantly different (Larson-Hall, 2010). The Mann-Whitney U test was used due to the small sample size and a concern for the data not being normally distributed.

3. Results and discussion

We first explored the type of CALL training and education instructors received. All the participants of the survey affirmed that they had been trained in the use of CALL. The survey revealed a considerable variety in the instructors' CALL training background. We classified these into two groups: the first group (G1), consisting of 13 instructors (46.4%), received CALL training as part of their MA or PhD as well as from in-service training, seminars, conferences, and lectures on CALL; the second group (G2) of 15 instructors (53.6%) only received CALL instruction as part of in-service training, seminars, conferences, and lectures on CALL.

We then examined instructors' perceptions towards their CALL training. Despite the varied CALL training backgrounds, the overall picture in terms of the perceived usefulness towards CALL training was very positive. The average mean score on the five-point Likert scale for all 13 items was 4.24 (SD=0.53) for G1 and 4.08 (SD=0.45) for G2. This showed that the participants of the two groups agreed that their CALL training helped them reflect, evaluate, select, use, and create computer-based instructional material. The Mann-Whitney U test showed that there was no significant difference (U=77.00, p=.699) between the two groups. When further investigated, individual items also showed no significant differences between G1 and G2 except for *Create computer-based instructional materials,* where the two groups significantly differed. Table 1 presents the results of instructors' perceptions towards received CALL training.

Table 1. Descriptive statistics and Mann-Whitney U test results of instructors' perceptions towards received CALL training

	Group 1 (N=13)		Group 2 (N=15)		Mann-Whitney U test	
	M	SD	M	SD	U-value	p-value
Reflect on your teaching practices with technologies.	4.31	0.63	4.21	0.80	88.5	.891
Evaluate computer-based instructional material.	4.15	0.80	3.79	0.89	70.5	.292
Make decisions regarding the selection of software for instruction.	4.15	0.80	3.93	0.73	76.0	.435
Make effective decisions regarding the use of technology for instruction.	4.38	0.65	3.93	0.62	57.5	.069
Use new technologies for language instruction.	4.62	0.65	4.29	0.61	63.0	.127
Use computer-based material for teaching the four language skills.	4.31	0.85	3.77	1.17	61.5	.210

Use course management systems (e.g. Blackboard, Moodle, etc.)	4.00	1.00	4.43	0.51	71.0	.291
Use new technologies to interact with your students.	4.38	0.65	4.43	0.51	90.0	.956
Use new technologies with your students to create collaborative learning projects.	4.08	0.86	3.93	1.00	85.0	.750
Create computer-based instructional materials.	4.46	0.66	4.00	0.55	55.0	.050*
Design technology-enhanced learning activities for your students.	4.38	0.51	4.07	0.73	70.0	.252
Facilitate learning rather than teaching directly.	4.31	0.63	4.21	0.70	85.0	.746
Teach your students to select appropriate software to improve their language skills.	3.69	1.11	3.64	1.28	90.5	.979

Note: * difference between means is at $p \leq .05$.

The data obtained indicate that the highest mean was reported in *Use new technologies for language instruction* followed by *Create computer-based instructional materials* for G1; for G2 this is represented by *Use course management systems* and *Use new technologies to interact with your students*. Interestingly, these are the only two items where G2's mean score is higher than G1's. By contrast, in the rest of the questions, G1 instructors present a higher mean in their perceptions towards the usefulness of the training received. In the opposite direction, *Teach your students to select appropriate software to improve their language skills* was the item with the lowest mean for both groups (slightly above 3.5). This shows that participants did not perceive that their training prepared them to foster autonomous learning with the use of technologies.

Additional analyses were performed to identify to what extent teachers' CALL education and professional development affect CALL practices; in particular, we were interested in examining hardware and specific software usage per semester. The overall mean of scores as a combined measure was

3.31 (*SD*=0.62) for G1 and 2.90 (*SD*=0.84) for G2 on the five-point Likert scale that ranged from *never* to *always*. This indicates that participants of the first group generally used technology in their classes slightly above the midpoint in the scale ('once per month') and the second group slightly below that point. In addition, a Mann-Whitney U test was conducted to determine whether there were differences between groups in hardware and software usage. Results of that analysis indicated that there was no significant difference between G1 and G2 (U=57.00, p=.062). However, when we further analysed individual items in order to identify areas where the two groups could differ, we found significant differences in the use of *mobile devices, website creators, wikis, photo-graphic software*, and *dictionaries*: G1 showed higher familiarity with using these items for language learning/teaching purposes than G2. Provided in Table 2 are the summary of means, standard deviations, and the results for the Mann-Whitney U test for the 21 items that measured the frequency of using hardware and software in the class.

Table 2. Descriptive statistics and Mann-Whitney U test results of instructors' usage of technology in their classes per semester

	Group 1 (N = 13)		Group 2 (N = 15)		Mann-Whitney U test	
	M	SD	M	SD	U-value	p-value
Computer	5.00	0.00	4.73	0.80	84.5	.180
Mobile devices	3.46	1.39	2.13	1.36	49.0	.021*
Projector	4.92	0.28	4.93	0.26	96.5	.918
Interactive whiteboard	2.54	1.61	1.87	1.64	75.0	.237
Word processor	4.69	0.63	4.27	1.16	79.0	.302
Presentation	4.23	0.73	4.40	0.91	79.5	.363
Internet browsers	4.92	0.28	4.40	1.06	71.5	.094
Cloud storage services	3.92	1.44	3.47	1.77	88.5	.659
Website creators	3.31	1.44	2.20	1.26	53.5	.036*
Blogs	2.85	1.46	1.93	1.22	58.0	.059
Wikis	2.77	1.54	1.67	1.05	52.5	.029*
E-learning platforms	4.31	1.03	4.00	1.31	84.0	.495
Social Media	3.54	1.85	2.87	1.68	76.0	.298
Audio/Music programmes	3.92	1.50	2.87	1.60	59.5	.069

Photo-Graphic programmes	2.69	1.38	1.67	1.40	45.0	.010*
Video editing software	2.31	0.95	2.00	1.51	68.0	.153
Instant messaging	1.92	1.32	1.67	1.18	85.5	.529
Video chat	2.08	1.55	2.00	1.25	96.5	.959
Translators	3.00	1.73	2.47	1.60	78.0	.350
Dictionaries	4.31	1.18	3.13	1.51	47.0	.014*
Games	3.15	1.41	2.33	1.29	63.0	.103

Note: * difference between means is at p≤.05.

Table 2 shows that of the four different devices listed in the survey, *computer* followed by *projector* were the most used by respondents of the two groups, who reported that they 'always' use them in their classes. In the opposite direction, the *interactive whiteboard* was the less used, though while the mean for G1 used it in the mid-point between 'once per term' and 'once per month', G2 used it slightly below 'once per term'. It is noteworthy that this item is not only related to CALL education but also to the technical infrastructure at their working place. This is not the case for the use of *mobile devices,* where we found significant differences between the groups. G1 used it between 'once per month' and 'once per week', G2 slightly used it above of 'once per term'. Concerning software usage, the most used by both groups (above 'once per week') were *internet browsers* followed by *word processors, e-learning platforms* and *presentations. Cloud storage services, audio programmes,* and *dictionaries* are also one of the most used software by G1 but not G2. Similarly, G1 also tended to use *blogs, social media, translators* and *games* 'once per month', yet for these four items participants of G2 responded that they use them below that frequency. Among the less used software in ascending order were *instant messaging, video chat,* and *video editing,* which both groups tended to use 'once per term'.

The data analysis depicted how HE L2 instructors perceived their CALL training. The survey responses showed that participants of both G1 and G2, regardless of their CALL education background, believed that their CALL training helped them to carry out CALL practices. However, besides this similarity in instructors' perceptions towards the training received, responses in terms of frequency of technology usage varied according to their CALL preparation. In general, G2 tended to use less frequently hardware and software than G1. Furthermore, significant differences were found in specific items, such as in the use of *wikis,* a database that can be developed collaboratively; yet both groups reported that their CALL training encouraged them to use new technologies with their students to create collaborative learning projects. The variation observed in instructors' beliefs and in their actual use of technology suggests that CALL training as part of MA or PhD programmes does make a difference, in other words, the knowledge and skills provided by these programmes are not obsolescent after instructors obtain certification (Guichon, 2009) nor impractical for pedagogical purposes (Kessler, 2007). Nonetheless, the results presented in this study reflected the frequency of technology usage, no differences can be reported on how the various technologies were used.

Finally, since the use of technology could be constrained by the working place characteristics, we also examined instructors' perceptions towards this factor. The results are presented in Table 3.

Table 3. Descriptive statistics and Mann-Whitney U test results of instructors' perceptions towards their working environment

	Group 1 (N=13)		Group 2 (N=15)		Mann-Whitney U test	
	M	SD	M	SD	U-value	p-value
A variety of computer software is available for use at my working place.	3.77	1.01	3.33	0.82	75.50	.286
The technical infrastructure at my working place is adequate.	3.31	1.32	3.33	1.11	96.50	.962
The technical support at my working place is adequate.	3.31	1.03	3.13	1.06	88.50	.664
The internet connection at my working place is adequate.	3.62	1.04	3.47	1.13	93.00	.829

The CALL training received did not seem to affect the instructors' attitudes with regards to their working place. No significant differences were found in this respect. Moreover, the four individual items in this measure had a mean score above three and below four for both groups, representing the neutral point on the Likert scale. However, each item is also characterised by a high standard deviation, indicating that participants of each group differed in their perceptions towards this factor. A possible explanation for this is that instructors belonged to different institutions, where the integration of CALL in language programmes varied according to university guidelines (Papadima-Sophocleous & Parmaxi, 2016) as well as the availability of resources and access to technology (Athanasiou & Nicolaou, 2014).

4. Conclusions

This study focussed on exploring CALL practices in the HE system in the Republic of Cyprus, and CALL education as one of the factors affecting those practices. The results of our survey showed different backgrounds in CALL education that did not affect instructors' attitudes towards the CALL training received. In general, the participants of the study agreed that their CALL preparation helped them to achieve pedagogical uses of technology. Yet, significant differences were found on the use of mobile devices and specific software between instructors who had formal and informal CALL preparation and those with only informal CALL preparation. These findings suggest that the knowledge and skills provided by MA or PhD programmes contribute to teaching with technologies at a higher level than informal CALL training. However, the degree of this contribution was lower than we expected, since significant differences in technology use for teaching purposes were only found in five items of the 21 listed in our survey.

In this exploration, the relevance of our study should be understood as illustrative rather than definitive. Our findings cannot be generalised to the whole population of language instructors in the Republic of Cyprus. Instead, the results should be taken as a description of CALL practices related to HE instructors with a particular CALL training background. In addition, since the study was conducted by a web-based interface, it could be possible that responses only represent those who are technology inclined. Future researchers may recruit a larger sample of participants to offer additional perspectives. It could also be possible that some instructors responded in technologically desirable ways. Because of this, we suggest that follow-up research should also examine CALL practices through observation. Despite these limitations, the findings of the study contribute to a better understanding of Cypriot HE L2 instructors' profiles, their CALL education, their beliefs about their CALL training, and their current CALL practices.

Acknowledgements

We would like to thank all the instructors that anonymously participated in the survey.

References

Athanasiou, A., & Nicolaou, A. (2014). Technology in language teaching: perceptions and experiences of university instructors. In M. Dodigovic (Ed.), *Attitudes to technology in ESL/EFL pedagogy*. TESOL Arabia Publications.

Debski, R. (2006). Theory and practice in teaching project-oriented CALL. In P. Hubbard & M. Levy (Eds), *Teacher education in CALL* (pp. 99-114). John Benjamins. https://doi.org/10.1075/lllt.14.10deb

Dörnyei, Z. (2010). *Questionnaires in second language research: construction, administration, and processing*. Routledge.

Ertmer, P., & Ottenbreit-Leftwich, A. (2010). Teacher technology change. How knowledge, beliefs, and culture intersect. *Journal of Research on Technology in Education, 42*(3), 221-251. https://doi.org/10.1080/15391523.2010.10782551

Georgina, D., & Hosford, C. C. (2009). Higher education faculty perceptions on technology integration and training. *Teaching and Teacher Education, 25*(5), 690-696. https://doi.org/10.1016/j.tate.2008.11.004

Guichon, N. (2009). Training future language teachers to develop online tutors' competence through reflective analysis. *ReCALL, 21*(2), 166-185. https://doi.org/10.1017/S0958344009000214

Hong, K. (2010). CALL teacher education as an impetus for L2 teachers in integrating technology. *ReCALL, 22*(1), 53-69. https://doi.org/10.1017/S095834400999019X

Hubbard, P., & Levy, M. (2006). The scope of CALL education. In P. Hubbard & M. Levy (Eds.), *Teacher education in CALL* (pp. 3-20). John Benjamins. https://doi.org/10.1075/lllt.14

Kessler, G. (2006). Assessing CALL teacher training: what are we doing and what could we do better? In P. Hubbard & M. Levy (Eds), *Teacher education in CALL* (pp. 23-43). John Benjamins. https://doi.org/10.1075/lllt.14.05kes

Kessler, G. (2007). Formal and informal CALL preparation and teacher attitude toward technology. *Computer Assisted Language Learning, 20*(2), 173-188. https://doi.org/10.1080/09588220701331394

Larson-Hall, J. (2010). *A guide to doing statistics in second language research using SPSS*. Routledge.

Lin, C.-Y., Huang, C.-K.,. & Chen, C.-H. (2014). Barriers to the adoption of ICT in teaching Chinese as a foreign language in US universities. *ReCALL, 26*(1), 100-116. https://doi.org/10.1017/S0958344013000268

Papadima-Sophocleous, S., & Parmaxi, A. (2016). Cyprus language centres: profiles and survival strategies in an era of diminishing resources. *INTED2016 conference*. https://doi.org/10.21125/inted.2016.1164

Papanastasiou, E.C., & Angeli, C. (2008). Evaluating the use of ICT in education: psychometric properties of the survey of factors affecting teachers teaching with technology (SFA-T). *Educational Technology & Society, 11*(1), 69-86.

Papayianni, M. (2012). *An investigation into English language teachers' CALL use in secondary education in Cyprus, their beliefs about using technology in teaching, and the factors that influence EFL teachers' CALL use*. Unpublished doctoral dissertation. University of Exeter.

Reinders, H. (2009). Teaching (with) technology: the scope and practice of teacher education for technology. *Prospect, 24*(3), 15-23.

Son, J., & Windeatt, S. (2017). *Language teacher education and technology: approaches and practices*. Bloomsbury Academic.

Vrasidas, C. (2015). The rhetoric of reform and teachers' use of ICT. *British Journal of Educational Technology, 46*(2), 370-380. https://doi.org/10.1111/bjet.12149

Yu, W., Sun, Y., & Chang, Y. (2010). When technology speaks language: an evaluation of course management systems used in a language learning context. *ReCALL, 22*(3), 332-355. https://doi.org/10.1017/S0958344010000194

3. Promoting pre-service teachers' inquiry skills in a blended model

Sandra Morales[1], Sandra Flores[2], and Claudia Trajtemberg[3]

Abstract

Lesson observation has been used with pre- and in-service teachers to improve classroom practices. In addition, reflection and criticality can be developed when teachers use evidence from their lessons and engage in collaborative discussions. Therefore, it is essential for pre-service teachers to collect data from their practices and reflect upon them individually and as a part of a teaching community. Thus, classroom-based studies in which blended models promote reflective research skills based on pedagogical practices are needed. Bearing this in mind, the aim of our case study was to examine the development of reflective inquiry skills amongst pre-service teachers in an English language teaching programme in Chile. We implemented a blended model of face-to-face sessions and an online community to foster discussions about classroom related issues. The face-to-face interactions took place as part of the Applied Research (AR) in teaching English as a foreign language course. The pre-service teachers' videos from the Practicum I (PI) course were uploaded onto the Video Enhanced Observation (VEO) online portal where self, peer, and teacher observation occurred. Data were collected from a questionnaire, comments on the VEO platform and focus groups. Statistical analyses were carried out using R scripts and quantitative content analyses were conducted with word clouds.

1. Universidad Diego Portales, Santiago, Chile; smoralesrios@gmail.com

2. Universidad de Chile, Santiago, Chile; Sfloresa87@gmail.com

3. Universidad Diego Portales, Santiago, Chile; claudiate@gmail.com

How to cite this chapter: Morales, S., Flores, S., & Trajtemberg, C. (2019). Promoting pre-service teachers' inquiry skills in a blended model. In C. N. Giannikas, E. Kakoulli Constantinou & S. Papadima-Sophocleous (Eds), *Professional development in CALL: a selection of papers* (pp. 39-53). Research-publishing.net. https://doi.org/10.14705/rpnet.2019.28.869

A thematic analysis was performed for the focus groups. Our findings suggest that the pre-service teachers' experiences in the blended model promoted their understanding of pedagogical issues and their capacity to address them as they embarked on research.

Keywords: pre-service language teachers, VEO, blended learning, reflection, inquiry skills.

1. Introduction

Language teachers should engage in constant professional development to meet the pedagogical needs of students who live in a rapidly changing world. It is essential that teachers develop teaching and reflective skills to identify issues in the classroom which lead to innovations. To foster teachers' reflections, videos have been used for lesson observation at both initial and continuous professional development (Sherin & Van Es, 2005; VEO Europa Project, www.veoeuropa.com). The process of self and peer observation allows pre-service and in-service teachers to detect teaching problems and solve them via reflection. In addition, mobile technology has facilitated lesson observation. Also, as online communities proliferate, teachers and teacher students engage more in social media for professional development (Lord & Lomicka, 2014). Mann and Walsh (2017) suggest that teachers should use evidence from their lessons to develop reflective skills. They indicate that "[d]ata-led accounts are essential since they provide the kind of evidence which promotes understandings of reflection" (Mann & Walsh, 2017, p. 17). We argue, thus, that to educate critical pre-service teachers, it is necessary to promote inquiry skills that help them to reflect and solve classroom issues effectively.

Reflection is encouraged in the English language teaching programme at Universidad Diego Portales (Chile) but emphasised in the students' PI course. Here, the students' teaching is observed and discussed with a mentor teacher. However, the students' ability to critically observe, reflect, and, mostly, provide concrete suggestions for a specific classroom related issue materialises when they design their research projects in the AR in English as a foreign language course prior to their thesis completion. The goal of our study, therefore, was to determine how reflective thinking skills were promoted, so teacher students develop a 'critical eye' in order to produce a research proposal. We implemented a blended model which included the face-to-face lessons in the AR course plus an online community using the VEO platform (www.veo-group.com).

2. Conceptual framework

Our study took a socio-constructivist stance as we considered the views of Dewey (1933). He suggests that inquiry is a process in which individuals analyse a situation of puzzlement and aim to solve it. He states that reflective thinking is developed by discussing, creating hypotheses, and eventually testing them. Dewey (1933) argues that reflection requires individuals to be open-minded, responsible, and enthusiastic. For educators, this means that they should be predisposed not only to provide constructive ideas and feedback, but also to receive them with an open mind. Therefore, the reflective thinking cycle to promote inquiry is supported by a teacher's experience, attitude, and belief.

We also drew on socio-cultural perspectives where social interaction is key as a means of supporting learning through collaboration. Consequently, it is important for students to reflect both individually and as part of a 'community of inquiry'. Lipman (1991) suggests that in communities of inquiry, individuals challenge truths and seek for meaning through dialogue and critical analysis. Collaborative learning has also been implemented in online learning. For instance, authors Garrison, Anderson, and Archer (2001) propose an approach for promoting reflection online, based on the work of Dewey (1933). They consider the members of the community, the interactions and the teacher as essential for learning to take place in an online environment. The online community model has been widely implemented with pre-service and in-service teachers to promote technology-mediated teacher education (Morales & Windeatt, 2015; Pawan, Paulus, Yalcin, & Chang, 2003).

Interactional and socio-constructivist approaches are essential to promote reflective thinking and classroom awareness amongst language teachers. Mann and Walsh (2017) consider the perspectives of Dewey (1933) and Vygotsky (1978) as fundamental for teachers' reflective skills development. In order to foster such reflection and interaction, video recordings of lessons can provide rich evidence for teachers to analyse individually and collaboratively. Van Es and Sherin (2002) acknowledge the benefits of videos in education and propose the concept of *noticing*. This means that teachers can detect relevant aspects of their teaching and analyse them. The authors highlight three essential elements for effective noticing:

> "(a) identifying what is important or noteworthy about a classroom situation; (b) making connections between the specifics of classroom interactions and the broader principles of teaching and learning they represent; and (c) using what one knows about the context to reason about classroom interactions" (Van Es & Sherin, 2002, p. 4).

The socio-constructivist view of our study was not only aligned with the theoretical framework, but also with our methodological choices. The quantitative and qualitative data we collected showed us how the participants worked on the blended model to enhance their inquiry skills and their perceptions about the process.

3. Methodology

We adopted the exploratory case study strategy for research design and mixed methods of data collection and analysis. Our research question was: how can inquiry skills be promoted for an effective design of a research project in the AR course?

The purpose of a case study is to investigate a phenomenon in its context to gain in-depth understanding of such phenomenon (Gomm, Hammersley, & Foster, 2000; Yin, 2003). Because this was a small-scale exploratory research, we believed that our main question should be broad enough to allow for data to emerge. Therefore, the case study allowed us to analyse how pre-service teachers developed their inquiry and reflective skills in a contextualised manner. In order to answer our research question, quantitative data were gathered using pre- and post-questionnaires to examine the students' perceptions on video-based lesson observation. Statistical analysis for the questionnaires was carried out through R scripts (https://www.R-project.org/). Also, the participants' comments on the VEO platform were quantified and analysed with word clouds (McNaught & Lam, 2010) to identify recurring words. Qualitative data were collected from focus groups and analysed using thematic analysis. The information from the quantitative and qualitative data set helped us to better understand the students' processes from different angles.

3.1. Context and participants

The study was conducted in an English language teaching programme at Universidad Diego Portales, Chile, between August and December 2017. The participants were 12 fourth year students, seven females and five males, enrolled in the AR and PI courses.

3.2. Methods and implementation

A blended model was implemented in the AR course; face-to-face lessons and the VEO platform. VEO is a mobile app created for reflective teacher professional development. Its customisable tag system allows teachers to identify and label relevant moments in their lessons. VEO also has a portal where participants can upload videos, share them, and exchange ideas. Considering the socio-constructivist approach of our study, VEO secured a space for meaningful online learning. In other studies (Batlle & Miller, 2017; Çelik, Baran, & Sert, 2018) VEO has been used to examine teacher observation practices and the role of different modes of teacher observation tools for peer feedback. In our study, the participants worked in dyads for the observation process. They were required to upload three recorded lessons from their PI course onto the VEO portal. They had to watch the videos and give each other feedback using a reflection template[4]. They also had to self-reflect on their performance. The teachers from the PI (Teacher 1) and AR courses together with the main researcher (Teacher 2) commented on the videos. The face-to-face lessons in the AR course served to link research related content (e.g. the problem statement, research questions) to the participants' teaching experiences in the PI.

3.3. Data collection and analysis

To answer our research question, we collected data regarding:

- the participants' views and comments about the use of VEO;

- the usefulness of the blended model; and

- the participants' views about the link between AR, PI, and VEO.

Evidence was gathered through questionnaires, the online community, and focus groups. We used frequencies, correlations, Multiple Correspondence Analysis (MCA) and a Kruskal-Wallis test for the quantitative data. We ran the Cronbach's alpha test for validity and reliability. Word clouds, MCAs, and graphs were applied as visualisation strategies. Qualitative data was categorised in themes with thematic analysis (Table 1).

Table 1. Summary of data collection and analysis

Instrument	Raw data	Method of analysis	Visualisation technique
Online questionnaire	24 answers in two applications of the questionnaire of 12 questions each, Likert scale	• Cronbach's alpha • Answer frequency • Spearman correlation • MCA • Kruskal-Wallis test	• Graphs • MCA

---

4. See supplementary material: https://research-publishing.box.com/s/27xpp3xm4ni3xdagu21d7j3sw4mfyi6x

VEO platform	83 comments written on VEO separated between students and teachers	• Quantitative content analysis per word frequency	• Word Cloud
Focus groups	Verbatim transcription	• Quantitative content analysis per word frequency • Qualitative thematic analysis	• Word Cloud

We adapted a questionnaire about videos for teacher professional development from Harvard University's 'Best Foot Forward' project (https://cepr.harvard.edu/best-foot-forward-project). The questionnaire was sent to the students on the first and last sessions of the AR course. The application of this instrument sought to explore the students' experiences using self-recorded video lessons. It included questions such as: *To what extent do you oppose or support video in addition to at least one in-person observation?* It had 12 Likert and three open ended questions. The latter were not considered in the analysis. The students' answers were brief; therefore, recurring patterns were not identified. Likert question number six was eliminated because its phrasing was unclear.

The internal consistency of the instrument was measured with Cronbach's alpha. A descriptive analysis of answer frequency per question was performed. Considering that sample size was lower than the number of questions (i.e. categorical variables), MCA analysis (Michailidis & de Leeuw, 1998) was carried out to detect the presence of an association among the questions, if any, between the answers expected after our model and the answers given by each of the students (observed answers). To assess the level of concordance between the pre- and post-questionnaires, we calculated the Spearman's rank correlation coefficient. The statistical significance of the differences between both sets of data was calculated applying a Kruskal-Wallis test.

Concerning the interactions in VEO, we conducted a word cloud analysis (McNaught & Lam, 2010). This examination showed us the most frequent concepts and/or words used by the members of the online community (see results). It also helped us to identify the nature of the reflection in which the students and teachers engaged.

The focus groups were conducted in Spanish and the questions we used were:

- What do you think of the use of VEO and the tags?

- How do you perceive VEO and its link with the PI and AR courses?

Transcription of the focus groups was carried out verbatim and a quantitative content analysis with word clouds (McNaught & Lam, 2010) was performed. The emerging patterns were displayed for the analysis, showing word size and frequency in the data. A thematic analysis was carried out by two of the researchers.

Lastly, the complete data set was contrasted against the final evaluation rubric of the AR course to determine how the blended model promoted critical reflection.

4. Results

The questionnaires had high internal reliability with a Cronbach's alpha of 0.78. When comparing both questionnaires, the Spearman's rho (i.e. used to observe association of variables) was of 0.9074. This showed a strong correlation between them and was consistent with MCA results that showed little variation between pre- and post-questionnaire responses.

When analysing the questions, 83.3% of the students answered *yes* (Figure 1) to Question 3: *Can you identify a specific change in your teaching practice you made as a result of the observation process this year?* This indicates that their experience in the blended model contributed to their development as pre-service teachers and the centrality of observation in promoting reflection. Also, when asked about the types of observation evidence that was most helpful for them, most students preferred video recordings of classrooms than, for example, teacher's notes or peers'/supervisors' notes.

Figure 1. Question 3 results

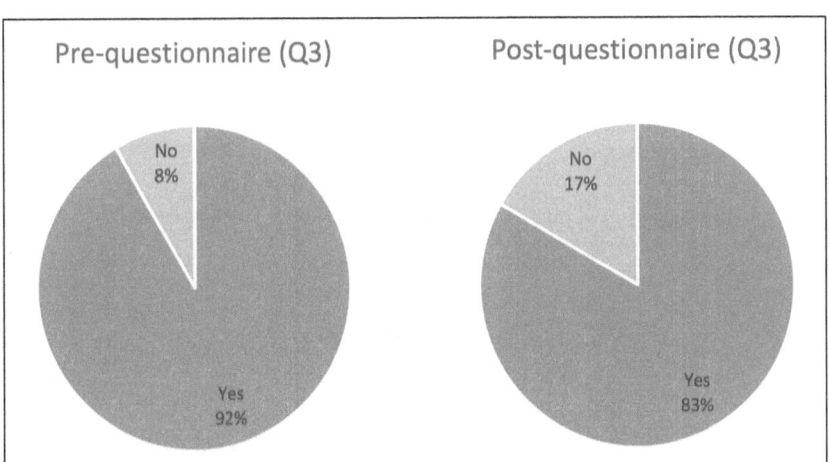

The VEO platform data set included 44 comments – self-reflection and peer feedback from the students and 39 from the teachers. Table 2 shows the number of comments. These comments were analysed quantitatively with word clouds. Figure 2 illustrates the total of all the words used in the three videos on VEO. Words such as 'students', 'class', 'instructions', 'good', and 'activity' predominated in the corpus produced by the community.

Table 2. Number of self-reflection comments, peer and teacher feedback on VEO

Video 1			Video 2			Video 3		
Student reflection	Peer comment	Teacher comment	Student reflection	Peer comment	Teacher comment	Student reflection	Peer comment	Teacher comment
12	8	11 PI1[5] 11 PI2[6]	9	6	5 PI1 5 PI2	8	1	7[7] MR[8]

---

5. One comment was sent via email.

6. One comment was sent via email.

7. The other two teachers sent three comments via email.

8. Main researcher

Figure 2. VEO interactions word cloud graph

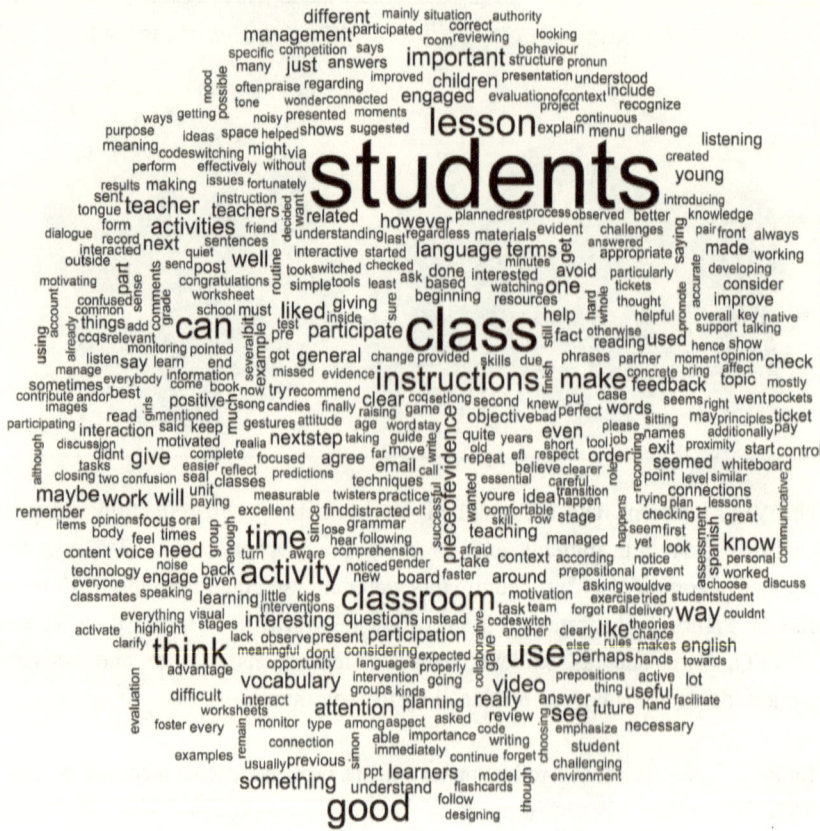

Regarding the focus group, the analysis allowed us to determine which concepts were more prominent and observe emerging patterns. The thematic analysis shows that the observation cycle was highly beneficial for the pre-service teachers' metacognitive process. As they observed and discussed their lessons in a safe online environment, they felt comfortable to share their views. In this sense, when watching their videos, they started thinking about the outcomes of the lesson and making connections with what they know about language teaching. One of the students explained that, due to lesson observation, she started thinking about the use of technology for language teaching. Another student stated that by seeing how children used games in class, he realised that this could be his research topic.

The participants stated that giving and receiving feedback in the platform was difficult. Watching the videos and writing feedback was time consuming. Additionally, there were times when they received delayed feedback (or no feedback) from all the teachers. In response to this, the teachers said that the delays in, and lack of, feedback was due to high workload and time constraints. Another limitation for the students was the use of the tags and the reflective template. They explained that they had always had 'freestyle' reflection in their courses, so they felt that using predetermined criteria was restrictive. In terms of having linked the PI and AR courses, the students commented that it was useful as their videos were used in both courses, but they stated that they felt confused at times about the activities they had to do for each course. For instance, other reflective tasks were conducted in the PI that did not involve VEO. Despite these challenges, the students expressed the view that discussing their videos was helpful for their teacher training and their research projects.

The pre-service teachers' final evaluation was considered in our analysis, as it served as a valid mediation tool. Table 3 shows upon which parameters the students were assessed, and how many students achieved each performance level. Each parameter earned three points, so for a student to get a full grade, they needed 24 points. The final evaluation was also preceded by presentations and discussions that stemmed from the community of inquiry.

Table 3. Final evaluation rubric

	Exceeds expectations	**Meets expectations**	**Approaches expectations**	**Below expectations**
Research problem	6	6		
Literature review	2	10		
Research questions	10	2		
Rationale and coherence	2	10		
Methodology	2	10		

References	4	8		
Structure and organisation	6	6		
Grammar and Vocabulary	2	8	2	

To illustrate the students' performance level, Table 3 shows the number of students per level. For example, 50% of the students managed to state a research problem that exceeded expectations, while 50% met the expectations. These percentages indicate how well the students managed to develop reflective inquiry skills to identify a classroom problem and produce research questions and a research proposal.

5. Discussion

Overall, the pre-service teachers perceived their experience with the blended model positively. Dewey (1933) suggests that reflective thinking is triggered by the identification of a problem that needs to be solved. In our study, the pre-service teachers' interactions fostered their knowledge about teaching and supported the development of criticality. The results of the questionnaires show that there was not a significant variation in the students' perceptions about using videos in their training. This indicates that they were aware of the usefulness of videos for lesson observation prior to our study. The reason, perhaps, was that they had been using videos in their PI course, so they were familiar with such visual resources. Nevertheless, they perceived that video recording was the most helpful type of observation evidence. In the blended model, they were able to use videos in an integrative manner for a research oriented rather than purely pedagogical purpose.

The videos were key in promoting reflection and discussion in the blended model. This is in line with what Mann and Walsh (2017) suggest regarding using authentic data to promote reflective practice. In our study, students had evidence to reflect upon from different perspectives. They were also able to re-watch their videos on VEO. This is particularly important as when observations are conducted live there might be aspects of the teaching that could go unnoticed. Also, in the virtual environment, members provided opportunities to engage in dialogue at any time. These ongoing interactions allowed pre-service teachers to think critically about ideas for their research projects. Therefore, this process supported the students' skills to notice relevant episodes in a lesson as proposed by Van Es and Sherin (2002). The VEO platform was essential to develop the pre-service teachers' reflective skills as they co-constructed knowledge through video tagging and discussion. Çelik et al. (2018) found that VEO was useful for the teachers as they made meaning of their collaborative reflections. The authors suggest that VEO should be used in initial teacher education. As shown in our results with the visualisation of the words commonly used in VEO (e.g. students, class, activity), the pre-service teachers became aware of their teaching while fostering their reflective thinking.

The use of predetermined tags was challenging for our participants. Sometimes, they identified something that was not in the tags or were not sure about what tag to use according to what they saw in the recording. The teachers in the research by Batlle and Miller (2017) about teachers' perceptions of VEO stated that, even though they thought tags were essential for giving feedback, they were also limiting. Thus, their observations coincide with the students' experience in our study. This poses the question about the usefulness of the tag system as it seemed to have inhibited the reflective process. Mann and Walsh (2017) encourage a revitalisation of reflective practice, and technological innovations are of great support to it. However, considering our findings, reflection was somewhat undermined by the tags. Going forward, we encourage users to create their own tag sets collaboratively, considering their observation needs. As a result, reflection could be enhanced by reflecting about triggering reflection.

6. Conclusions

Our study aimed at supporting the development of reflective inquiry skills in a blended model amongst senior pre-service teachers in the English as a foreign language teaching programme at Universidad Diego Portales, Chile. We implemented a blended model that integrated reflection in face-to-face lessons (AR course) and an online community in the VEO portal. Our findings show that the pre-service teachers were able to identify issues from their teaching and produce a research proposal. This outcome suggests that the teacher students' work in the blended model supported their reflective skills. Therefore, we strongly suggest that such reflective experiences continue to be implemented in initial and continuous teacher education. It would be interesting to further observe the effectiveness of technological reflective tools and their impact on pre-and in-service teachers' reflections and teaching. We consider the experience of the pre-service teachers in this blended model as a starting point in their journey to become active reflective practitioners and researchers in their teaching communities.

Acknowledgements

This study was funded by the 'Proyectos de Innovación' grant from Vicerrectoría de Pregrado (VRP), Universidad Diego Portales, Chile. Special thanks to Paul Miller and Jon Haines from VEO Ltd, our participants (2014 cohort), and Practicum teachers.

References

Batlle, J., & Miller, P. (2017). Video enhanced observation and teacher development: teachers' beliefs as technology users. *EDULEARN17 Proceedings* (pp. 2352-2361). https://doi.org/10.21125/edulearn.2017.1487

Çelik, S., Baran, E., & Sert, O. (2018). The affordances of mobile-app supported teacher observations for peer feedback. *International Journal of Mobile and Blended Learning (IJMBL)*, *10*(2), 36-49. https://doi.org/10.4018/IJMBL.2018040104

Dewey, J. (1933). *How we think: a restatement of the relation of reflective thinking to the educative process.* D.C. Heath & Co Publishers.

Garrison, D. R., Anderson, T., & Archer, W. (2001). Critical thinking, cognitive presence, and computer conferencing in distance education. *American Journal of distance education*, *15*(1), 7-23. https://doi.org/10.1080/08923640109527071

Gomm, R., Hammersley, M., & Foster, P. (Eds). (2000). *Case study method: key issues, key texts*. SAGE.

Lipman, M. (1991). *Thinking in Education. The reflective model of educational practice*. Cambridge University Press.

Lord, G., & Lomicka, L. (2014). Twitter as a tool to promote community among language teachers. *Journal of Technology and Teacher Education, 22*(2), 187-212.

Mann, S., & Walsh, S. (2017). *Reflective practice in English language teaching: research-based principles and practices*. Routledge. https://doi.org/10.4324/9781315733395

McNaught, C., & Lam, P. (2010). Using Wordle as a supplementary research tool. *The qualitative report, 15*(3), 630.

Michailidis, G., & de Leeuw, J. (1998). The Gifi system of descriptive multivariate analysis. *Statistical Science, 13*(4), 307-336. https://doi.org/10.1214/ss/1028905828

Morales, S., & Windeatt, S. (2015). How language teachers become effective users of CALL for online teaching and learning: a case study of their developmental processes in a transformative e-training course. In A. Gimeno, M. Levy, F. Blin, & D. Barr (Eds), *WorldCALL: sustainability and computer-assisted language learning* (pp. 78-100). Bloomsbury.

Pawan, F., Paulus, T. M., Yalcin, S., & Chang, C. F. (2003). Online learning: patterns of engagement and interaction among in-service teachers. *Language Learning & Technology, 7*(3), 119-140.

Sherin, M. G., & Van Es, E. A. (2005). Using video to support teachers' ability to notice classroom interactions. *Journal of technology and teacher education, 13*(3), 475.

Van Es, E. A., & Sherin, M. G. (2002). Learning to notice: scaffolding new teachers' interpretations of classroom interactions. *Journal of Technology and Teacher Education, 10*(4), 571-596.

Vygotsky, L. S. (1978). *Mind in society*. Harvard University Press.

Yin, R. (2003). *Case study research: design and methods*. Sage.

4 Revisiting the cloud: reintegrating the G Suite for Education in English for Specific Purposes teaching

Elis Kakoulli Constantinou[1]

Abstract

In an era of continuous technological advancement and severe financial crisis, the cloud computing paradigm has become one of the most prominent and influential developments in information technology since the emergence of the Internet. This chapter describes the second phase of an action research study, which aimed at addressing the problem of lack of appropriate technology tools for the delivery of two blended English for Academic Purposes (EAP) courses for first-year students of the Departments of (1) Agricultural Sciences, Biotechnology, and Food Science and (2) Commerce, Finance, and Shipping, at the Cyprus University of Technology. The solution suggested involved the integration of the G Suite for Education[2] in the teaching and learning process. The suite was firstly introduced in the academic year 2016-2017 (Kakoulli Constantinou, 2018), and the feedback obtained then was valuable for its reintegration the following year. The present chapter focusses on the second attempt to integrate the suite in the context of which data was elicited in order to improve the use of the suite for the delivery of the two EAP courses in the future.

Keywords: cloud technologies, blended teaching, English for specific purposes, G Suite for Education.

1. Cyprus University of Technology, Limassol, Cyprus; elis.constantinou@cut.ac.cy

2. https://eduproducts.withgoogle.com/products/g-suite/g-suite-for-education

How to cite this chapter: Kakoulli Constantinou, E. (2019). Revisiting the cloud: reintegrating the G Suite for Education in English for Specific Purposes teaching. In C. N. Giannikas, E. Kakoulli Constantinou & S. Papadima-Sophocleous (Eds), *Professional development in CALL: a selection of papers* (pp. 55-69). Research-publishing.net. https://doi.org/10.14705/rpnet.2019.28.870

Chapter 4

1. Introduction

The utilisation of cloud computing services for educational purposes has started to encroach upon local 'hosting and operating resources', such as the ones offered at a school or a university network, due to the countless merits cloud computing encompasses (Khmelevsky & Voytenko, 2010, p. 1). There is an increasing number of educational institutions which opt for cloud computing services for several reasons that relate to the practical and economic advantages of this type of technology, but also because of its benefits for learning.

There are several definitions of cloud computing in the literature. Sultan (2010) describes it as "clusters of distributed computers (largely vast data centres and server farms) which provide on-demand resources and services over a networked medium (usually the Internet)" (p. 110). Cloud computing refers to both the applications/software offered on the Internet as well as the hardware and all the programming that occurs for these services to be provided. Such services provide easy access to different applications, which enable users to store, share, maintain, and generally manage material and communicate online from anywhere, using almost any device.

The present chapter concentrates on the use of the G Suite for Education in English for Specific Purposes (ESP). It reports on the second phase of an action research study conducted at the Cyprus University of Technology. The sections which follow provide a brief review on literature on cloud computing, information on the research context, and the results of the second attempt of the integration of the G Suite for Education in two ESP courses.

1.1. Using cloud computing services for educational purposes

According to Mell and Grance (2011), cloud computing is composed of five essential characteristics: (1) *on-demand self-service*, which refers to the ability of each user to manage computing services automatically; (2) *broad network access* that relates to the fact that services can be accessed from any place using any device (e.g. mobile phones, tablets, laptops, and workstations) as long as there is a reliable internet connection; (3) *resource pooling*, which involves resources that include storage, processing, memory, and network bandwidth being available at all times; (4) *rapid elasticity* due to which services are made automatically available to consumers, unlimited at any time; and (5) *measured service*, which concerns the ability of both the provider and the user to measure, monitor, and control the resources utilised.

Furthermore, apart from all these affordances that indirectly support the teaching and learning process, there is evidence in the literature that cloud computing contributes both directly and indirectly to the learning process (Arpaci, 2017; González-Martínez, Bote-Lorenzo, Gómez-Sánchez, & Cano-Parra, 2015). All of the above characteristics, in combination with other affordances of cloud computing, such as its cost effectiveness, ease of use, and high scalability, have made cloud computing one of the most prevailing technologies or 'key trends' in the technology-enhanced learning domain (Ercan, 2010; Lakshminarayanan, Kumar, & Raju, 2013; Sultan, 2010).

Notwithstanding all its advantages, cloud computing involves certain challenges and dangers, mostly related to issues of privacy and security (Dillon, Wu, & Chang, 2010; González-Martínez et al., 2015). The interest in such issues has started becoming more intense during the last year, especially with the introduction of the data protection and online privacy rules which apply to both companies and organisations (public and private) inside and outside the European Union[3]. These newly established regulations will hopefully reinforce security and data protection, minimising the concerns expressed by skeptics.

1.2. ESP and the G Suite for Education

ESP is a "broad and diverse field of English language teaching" that refers to "language programmes designed for groups or individuals who are learning

---

3. https://europa.eu/youreurope/citizens/consumers/internet-telecoms/data-protection-online-privacy/index_en.htm

with an identifiable purpose and clearly specified needs" (Johnson & Johnson, 1998, p. 105). In other words, as its name denotes, ESP relates to the study of English usually associated with a particular field of study or a particular profession, for example English for Business, English for Hotel and Tourism Management, etc. As in every language learning context, ESP learners need to be exposed to as much authentic English that relates to their field of study as possible, since authenticity enhances learners' motivation, promotes learner autonomy, and immerses the learners in real world language communication (Shuang, 2014).

With all its qualities and affordances, cloud computing could be one of the best tools to be integrated in an ESP class. The G Suite for Education is one of the most popular cloud-based productivity suites offered by Google, which includes Mail, Drive, Classroom, Docs, Sheets, Slides, Sites, Calendar, and other applications used by 70 million students and teachers (Fenton, 2017). The features and applications of the G Suite are praised by many researchers who stress the value of integrating the G Suite for Education in teaching and learning, elaborating on its ease of use and focussing on its affordances for collaboration, dissemination of material and information, organisation, and limitless storage (Florell, 2017; Herrick, 2009; Lindh, Nolin, & Hedvall, 2016; McCloud & Marinello, 2014). The suite can extend learning beyond the walls of the classroom and give the learners the opportunity to be exposed to real language use, which is fundamental not only in ESP in particular, but in language learning in general.

1.3. The context of the research

In fall 2016, the researcher, who was also the course facilitator, integrated the G Suite for Education in her teaching of two blended EAP courses at the Cyprus University of Technology, one for the Department of Commerce, Finance, and Shipping and another for the Department of Agricultural Sciences, Biotechnology, and Food Science. The suite was integrated in the courses as a solution to the problem of the lack of appropriate tools which ensure classroom management, saving, organising, and sharing material online and also allow for online collaboration and interaction between learners (Kakoulli Constantinou, 2018)

Both courses were at a B1-B2 level of the Common European Framework of Reference (CEFR) for languages, and in both cases language competence was acquired through the use of text types, scenarios, and roles which promoted the production and understanding of spoken and written language related to the topics covered. The courses were based on social constructivist theories, some elements of connectivism, and student-centred teaching methods. The G Suite applications that were utilised for the delivery of the courses were Google Classroom with all its features, serving as a platform for the course, and Google Drive with Google Docs, Google Slides, etc. for the creation (individual and collaborative), storage, and sharing of material. Furthermore, Google search was used in order to find information and materials on specific topics, and Gmail was employed for communication purposes. Finally, a closed Facebook group was created for each course for posting announcements, sharing material outside classes, commenting on different topics, and communicating with each other.

2. Method

Being an action research study, the study evolved in a spiral process of continuous improvement; the study commenced with the identification of a specific problem, that is the lack of efficient technology tools for classroom management and other educational processes, it proceeded with the provision of a solution through the integration of the G Suite in the two courses (fall 2016-2017), followed by reflection, refinement and repetition of the whole process the following year (fall 2017-2018). The present chapter reports on the results of the second cycle of the research study (fall 2017-2018).

2.1. Tools

Apart from the students' comments and the course facilitator's field notes kept during the courses, an online questionnaire, created using Google Forms, was administered to the students for purposes of reflection after the completion of the courses. The questionnaire consisted of 15 Likert-scale and open-ended questions. It was the same as the one used in Cycle 1 of the research study, and it aimed at obtaining data related to (1) the learners' profile, (2) the learners' perceptions on the G Suite for Education's ease of use, (3) the learners' perceptions on the efficiency of the G Suite for Education, and (4) general comments regarding the integration of the suite in the two courses.

The qualitative data obtained was analysed using thematic analysis, and quantitative data was analysed using the Statistical Package for Social Sciences (SPSS) version 22, and descriptive statistics were used to report on the results.

2.2. Participants

The sample was comprised of 65 first year students: 33 from the Department of Agricultural Sciences, Biotechnology, and Food Science, and 32 from Commerce, Finance, and Shipping. All participants had common linguistic backgrounds with Greek being their native language. Table 1 describes the profiles of the participants in the study.

Table 1. The participants

	N=65	%
Departments		
• Agricultural Sciences, Biotechnology, and Food Science	33	50.8
• Commerce, Finance, and Shipping	32	49.2
Sex		
• Female	32	49.2
• Male	33	50.8
Age		
• 17-20	59	90.8
• 21-24	5	7.7
• 25-30	1	1.5
Origin		
• Cypriot	63	96.9
• Greek	2	3.1

3. Results and discussion

3.1. The participants' profile

At the beginning of the courses, in order for the researcher to have a comprehensive view of the profile of the participants, students were asked to state whether they were familiar with Google applications; their comments revealed that some students were not familiar with some applications, therefore the researcher ensured that they received the appropriate guidance they needed to be able to use the tools while the course was taking place. The results of Cycle 1 of the research study (Kakoulli Constantinou, 2018) had also indicated specific aspects of the course that the facilitator needed to pay closer attention to in the second integration of the suite in her courses (Cycle 2). Moreover, a question regarding students' level of familiarity with Google applications when they started the course was also included in the questionnaire, and the responses reinforced the initial findings. As illustrated in Figure 1, responses to this question ranged from not familiar at all (16.92%) to very familiar (23.08%), with the majority stating that they had little familiarity with Google applications (83.08%); this indicated that some of the students could have found the use of the suite more challenging than the rest (probably the ones who were not familiar with the applications at all, and the ones who were little familiar with the applications, 49.23%).

Figure 1. Students' familiarity with Google applications

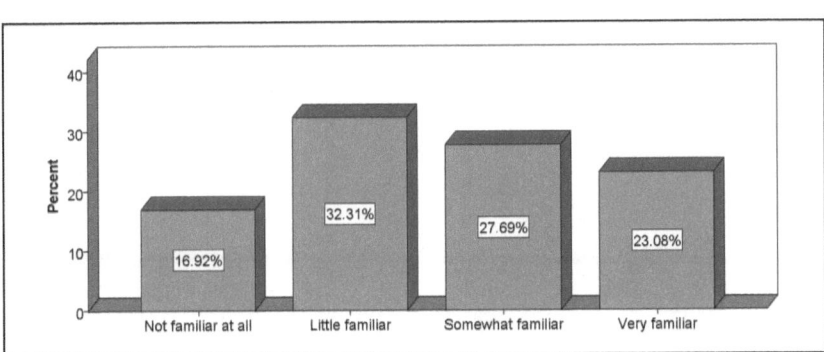

Chapter 4

3.2. G Suite for Education ease of use

Regarding learners' perceptions on the G Suite for Education's ease of use, students were requested to describe the use of Google Classroom, Google Drive, Gmail, and Google search, which were the main Google applications utilised for the delivery of the course. Students' comments during the course as well as the facilitator's field notes revealed that generally both students and the facilitator considered the suite as easy to use, facing only minor challenges during its use. Students' questionnaire responses, displayed in Figure 2, confirm this. Generally, students regarded the tools as easy to use, with Google search and Gmail being regarded as the easiest, probably because these are tools that students in Cyprus often use in their everyday life. It is interesting to note that none of the students responded that they considered the tools to be difficult to use, a fact that confirms Herrick's (2009) and Fenton's (2017) claim that simplicity is among the virtues of the suite.

Figure 2. G Suite for Education's ease of use

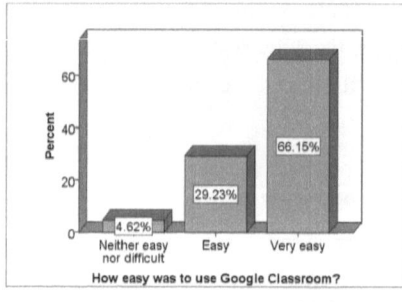
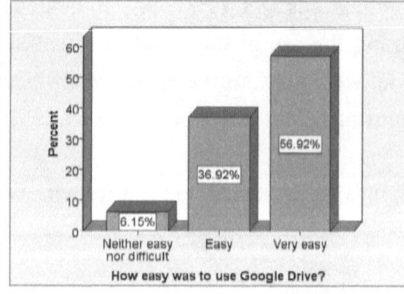
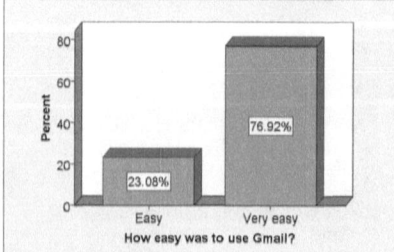
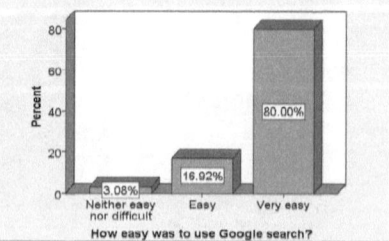

3.3. Challenges faced

Students were also asked to comment on the elements that they found challenging. The vast majority stated that they did not face any challenges with using the tools. The challenges that were reported by the students were the following:

> "I never used Google Classroom and Google Drive before, and I had to learn how to use them. One difficulty that I encountered was that I couldn't click on a button to save something on Google Drive, so sometimes I was afraid to close the window despite that I knew that my work would be saved without clicking on it" (EAP for Agricultural Sciences, Biotechnology, and Food Science student).

> "I just needed some time to get familiar with Google Classroom but after using it a couple of times I got used to it" (EAP for Agricultural Sciences, Biotechnology, and Food Science student).

> "Not being familiar with Google Drive" (EAP for Commerce, Finance, and Shipping student).

The fact that students did not encounter serious challenges with the use of the suite implies that the changes that the facilitator had introduced with the refinement of the courses (more guidance with the use of the tools, both face-to-face and also by means of written instructions uploaded on the Google Classroom platform) were effective.

3.4. G Suite for Education efficiency

Concerning the learners' perceptions on the efficiency of the G Suite for Education, results showed that in general all the tools used in the courses were regarded as efficient for their delivery. Students' questionnaire responses are presented in Table 2. Google Classroom was regarded as a very effective tool for various purposes, as listed in Table 2; however, it was considered as less efficient for commenting on different topics and seeing different announcements about the course. This was perhaps due to the fact that students were more active on the Facebook closed group that the facilitator had created for the course that they were attending. The present study did not examine the use of the Facebook closed group; nonetheless, a study conducted by Veira, Leacock, and Warrican (2014) showed that students seem to prefer using a Facebook wall for discussion and interaction over a Google group, most probably because today's students are regarded as 'digital natives' who are more familiar with the use of social media. Consequently, students' preference for social media could explain why a small percentage of students characterised Google Classroom as poor for commenting or posting announcements for the course.

Table 2. The efficiency of G Suite for Education tools

	Very poor %	Poor %	Acceptable %	Good %	Very good %
How good is Google Classroom for...					
serving as an online platform for the course?	-	-	3.1	35.4	61.5
keeping you informed about the topics and learning outcomes for each session every week?	-	-	10.8	27.7	61.5
providing you with material for the course (documents, videos, links, course outline, etc.)?	-	-	3.1	44.6	52.3
providing you with information about the instructor?	-	-	7.7	44.6	47.7
giving you instructions for each task?	-	-	4.6	46.2	49.2
uploading assignments?	-	1.5	7.7	26.2	64.6
viewing your grades?	-	-	9.2	29.2	61.5
commenting on different topics?	-	1.5	6.2	36.9	55.4
seeing different announcements about the course?	1.5	1.5	7.7	35.4	53.8
creating a feeling of belonging to a community?	-	-	13.8	29.2	56.9
How good is Google Drive (including Docs, Slides, etc.) for...					
writing notes/answers to tasks for each class?	-	-	13.8	35.4	50.8
creating assignments?	-	-	10.8	40	49.2

organising your files and keeping records of classes/storing files?	-	3.1	7.7	29.3	60
collaborating with classmates?	-	3.1	10.8	38.5	47.7
sharing material?	-	3.1	1.5	33.8	61.5
How good is Gmail for...					
communicating with the instructor?	-	-	9.2	26.2	64.6
communicating with classmates?	-	1.5	10.9	29.2	58.5
receiving feedback on the assignments?	-	-	6.2	30.8	63.1
How good is Google search for...					
finding information on different topics?	-	-	4.6	30.8	64.6
explaining unknown vocabulary?	-	1.5	9.2	33.8	55.4

3.5. G Suite for Education experience in general

As regards the general evaluation of the whole experience using the Suite, students' comments during the two courses, the facilitator's field notes, and their questionnaire responses revealed that students were satisfied with the whole experience. Figure 3 presents students' satisfaction with the whole G Suite experience, as expressed in their questionnaire responses. Their responses regarding the support that they received from the course facilitator were similar (Figure 4).

Some of the elements of the two EAP courses that were regarded as the most enjoyable by the students were the following:

- sharing work and collaborating with classmates;
- communicating through the platform (Google Classroom);
- working on assignments and group projects;
- watching the video clips that were uploaded on Google Classroom;
- working online;
- working on Google Classroom;
- using a PC during the lesson;

- cooperating with the course facilitator;
- using online dictionaries;
- using Google Drive and having everything stored on the cloud;
- using Gmail and Google search;
- the fact that the course was organised; and
- the hybrid use of digital and live teaching.

Figure 3.   Evaluation of the experience using the G Suite for Education

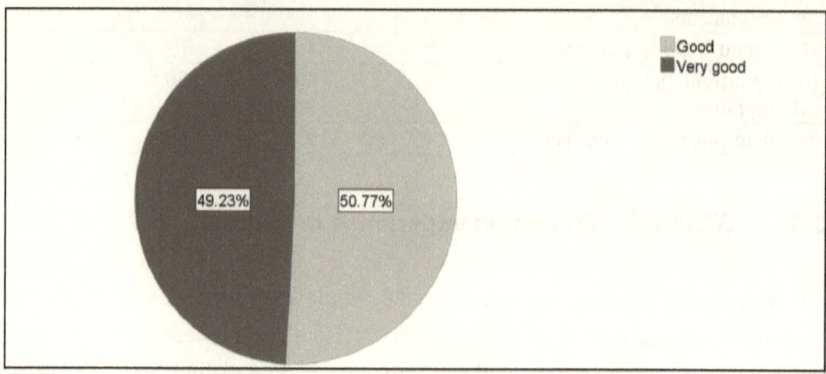

Figure 4.   The course facilitator's support

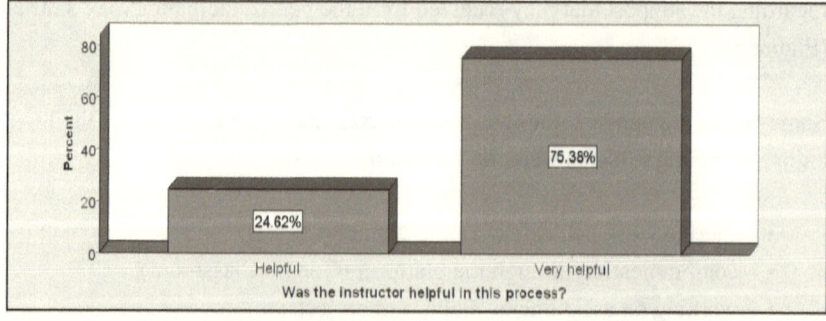

Students' satisfaction with the integration of the G Suite in their EAP course was also illustrated in their responses related to their wish to use these tools again in the future as summarised in Table 3.

Table 3. Students' wish to use the G Suite for Education in the future

Students' Responses	%
No	1.5
Yes	84.6
No response	13.8

4. Conclusions

Despite the fact that research in the use of cloud computing in education is still young, previous studies that have been conducted in the field concur that this type of technology is a very promising one and that it could constitute a 'new dawn' in education (Ercan, 2010; González-Martínez et al., 2015; Lakshminarayanan et al., 2013; Sultan, 2010). Cloud computing is practical, flexible, easy to use, cost effective, and offers high scalability. Moreover, with all of its affordances, which allow for interaction, communication, collaboration, finding, sharing, and storing material, it can support research and it can facilitate learning; according to the latest developments in the theories of learning which embrace social constructivist and connectivist approaches, learning is based very much on social interaction with the environment and networking, which means learning from each other. Such approaches can be catered for by cloud technologies, such as the G Suite for Education.

The study may have limitations, mostly related to the fact that action research is conducted with small samples and it operates in specific contexts trying to provide solutions to specific problems. For this reason, action research does not aim at generalisability but going in depth through iteration and the continuous cyclical process of improvement, which ensure quality and reduce subjectivity (Burns, 2005). Nevertheless, the study may yield some interesting insights pertaining to the use of cloud computing in general and the G Suite in particular that may prove useful to ESP educators, general English practitioners, teacher trainers, or even educational institutions who wish to adopt cloud technologies in the future.

The present study also generates ideas for future research. More specifically, it would be interesting to investigate how the integration of the Google Suite for Education evolves through the years; adopting new features and applications that the suite will offer in the future. Another parametre that would be useful for future research to examine would be to go beyond students' perceptions and assess how effective these tools are in the acquisition of the target language. Finally, future research in the field of cloud computing could also explore to what extent students in general continue using the specific tools for study or even in their everyday life after being initiated in the use of these technologies in the context of their studies.

References

Arpaci, I. (2017). Antecedents and consequences of cloud computing adoption in education to achieve knowledge management. *Computers in Human Behavior, 70*(2017), 382-390. https://doi.org/10.1016/j.chb.2017.01.024

Burns, A. (2005). Action research: an evolving paradigm? *Language Teaching, 38*(2), 57-74. https://doi.org/10.1017/S0261444805002661

Dillon, T., Wu, C., & Chang, E. (2010). Cloud computing: issues and challenges. *2010 24th IEEE International Conference on Advanced Information Networking and Applications*, (pp. 27-33). https://doi.org/10.1109/AINA.2010.187

Ercan, T. (2010). Effective use of cloud computing in educational institutions. *Procedia - Social and Behavioral Sciences, 2*(2), 938-942. https://doi.org/10.1016/j.sbspro.2010.03.130

Fenton, W. (2017, June 23). Google Classroom could bridge a gap in online learning. *PC Magazine*. https://www.pcmag.com/commentary/354491/google-classroom-could-bridge-a-gap-in-online-learning

Florell, D. (2017). Just a click away; G Suite for Education and school psychology. *Communiqué, 46*(3), 36.

González-Martínez, J. A., Bote-Lorenzo, M. L., Gómez-Sánchez, E., & Cano-Parra, R. (2015). Cloud computing and education: a state-of-the-art survey. *Computers and Education, 80*, 132-151. https://doi.org/10.1016/j.compedu.2014.08.017

Herrick, D. R. (2009). Google this! Using Google apps for collaboration and productivity. *Proceedings of the 37th Annual ACM SIGUCCS Fall Conference* (pp. 55-64).

Johnson, K., & Johnson, H. (1998). *Encyclopedic dictionary of applied linguistics*. Blackwell Publishers Ltd.

Kakoulli Constantinou, E. (2018). Teaching in clouds: using the G Suite for Education for the delivery of two English for Academic Purposes courses. *The Journal of Teaching English for Specific and Academic Purposes, 6*(2), Special Issue, 305-317. https://doi.org/10.22190/JTESAP1802305C

Khmelevsky, Y., & Voytenko, V. (2010). Cloud computing infrastructure prototype for university education and research categories and subject descriptors. *Computing*, 1-5. https://doi.org/10.1145/1806512.1806524

Lakshminarayanan, R., Kumar, B., & Raju, M. (2013). Cloud computing benefits for educational institutions. *Second International Conference of the Omani Society for Educational Technology, 8*, 104-112. http://arxiv.org/ftp/arxiv/papers/1305/1305.2616.pdf

Lindh, M., Nolin, J., & Hedvall, N. K. (2016). Pupils in the clouds: implementation of Google apps for education. *First Monday, 21*(4). https://doi.org/10.5210/fm.v21i4.6185

McCloud, M., & Marinello, N. (2014). Introducing classroom, a new tool in Google apps for education. *Sponsored Web Seminar Digest*, 52-54.

Mell, P., & Grance, T. (2011). *The NIST definition of cloud computing; recommendations of the national institute of standards and technology*. National Institute of Standards and Technology.

Shuang, L. (2014). Authenticity in language teaching. *Applied Mechanics and Materials, 543-547*, 4294-4297. https://doi.org/10.4028/www.scientific.net/AMM.543-547.4294

Sultan, N. (2010). Cloud computing for education: a new dawn? *International Journal of Information Management, 30*(2), 109-116. https://doi.org/10.1016/j.ijinfomgt.2009.09.004

Veira, A. K., Leacock, C. J., & Warrican, S. J. (2014). Learning outside the walls of the classroom: engaging the digital natives. *Australasian Journal of Educational Technology, 30*(2), 227-244. https://doi.org/10.14742/ajet.349

5 Do EFL teachers transform their teaching with iPads? A TPACK-SAMR approach

Jun-Jie Tseng[1]

Abstract

Over the past decade, there has been an increasing interest in research on teacher knowledge about technology integration, namely Technological Pedagogical Content Knowledge (TPACK). However, few studies have investigated how teachers transform their teaching with technology. To fill this gap, the present study adopted the Substitution, Augmentation, Modification, and Redefinition (SAMR) model to investigate the degree to which four Taiwanese English as a Foreign Language (EFL) teachers enacted their TPACK in the context of teaching English with iPads, as well as identified contextual factors that might influence the levels of their TPACK enactments. Results suggested that, although some of the teachers' iPad-based teaching indicated their competency in transforming their teaching, their teaching was predominantly enhanced by the tablets as a substitute to deliver linguistic input to their students in conventional teacher-centred classrooms. In addition, students' access to iPads and a wireless network was considered essential. This technological problem might constrain the teachers from enacting TPACK towards the higher levels of the SAMR scale. This study contributes to the literature on TPACK by providing empirical evidence on investigating the levels of TPACK enactments using the SAMR model.

Keywords: technological pedagogical content knowledge, SAMR, contextual factors, iPads.

---

1. English Department of National Taiwan Normal University, Taipei, Taiwan; jjtseng@ntnu.edu.tw

How to cite this chapter: Tseng, J.-J. (2019). Do EFL teachers transform their teaching with iPads? A TPACK-SAMR approach. In C. N. Giannikas, E. Kakoulli Constantinou & S. Papadima-Sophocleous (Eds), *Professional development in CALL: a selection of papers* (pp. 71-85). Research-publishing.net. https://doi.org/10.14705/rpnet.2019.28.871

Chapter 5

1. Introduction

1.1. iPads in EFL classrooms

Mobile technology has increasingly been applied to student learning in the classroom around the world. Student learning can be enhanced via a variety of apps, such as dictionaries, reading, writing, graphic organisers, note-taking, multimedia production, and communication. Within this framework of Mobile Assisted Language Learning (MALL), mobile technology can contribute to language development of vocabulary (Lin & Yu, 2017), grammar (Khodabandeh, Alian, & Soleimani, 2017), reading (Lin, 2014), listening (Hsu, 2015), speaking (Sun et al., 2017), and writing (Eubanks, Yeh, & Tseng, 2018). By embracing MALL, teachers demonstrate that they are keen to integrate mobile technology into their teaching (Hsu, 2016; Young, 2016). However, they face technological and pedagogical challenges when applying it to teaching practices (Burston, 2014). To address the issue within the current context, the present study created a teacher community in which four Taiwanese EFL teachers shared their ideas and discussed their experiences with peers about enhancing English teaching with iPads. In fact, this intervention involves the enactments of their knowledge about integrating iPads into teaching, i.e. teacher knowledge specifically known as TPACK, which is critical to the adoption of MALL (Hsu, 2016).

1.2. TPACK

TPACK was proposed by Mishra and Koehler (2006) to describe teacher knowledge in relation to integrating technology into teaching and learning. TPACK deals with how teachers develop their understanding of applying technology to the teaching of subject-matter content in an appropriate pedagogical manner. This process involves the interplay among the three bodies of core knowledge (i.e. technological knowledge, pedagogical knowledge, and content knowledge), as shown in Figure 1.

Investigating TPACK is a continuing concern within teacher education. Many researchers have been exploring how teachers enact and develop their TPACK (e.g. Hao, 2016; Hsu, 2016; Koehler, Mishra, & Yahya, 2007; Niess, 2011). For example, Hutchison, Beschorner, and Schmidt-Crawford (2012) investigated the possibility of enhancing literacy instructions with iPads. Oriented towards the TPACK model, a fourth-grade teacher was guided to examine how she achieved curriculum objectives in iPad-based teaching with concerns about using iPads to teach what content, in what pedagogical ways, and with what apps to support student learning. Consequently, it was found that iPads not only contributed to student engagement but also facilitated students to learn in unique, creative ways. This study revealed how the teacher applied her TPACK to teaching literacy with iPads. However, this line of TPACK research failed to indicate whether technology helped teachers transform their teaching. Little was known about the degree to which teachers transformed their teaching using technology. To address this problem, Puentedura's (2006) SAMR model was adopted in the present study because this framework could help differentiate the levels of four Taiwanese EFL teachers' TPACK enactments in their iPad-based English teaching.

Figure 1. TPACK model[2]

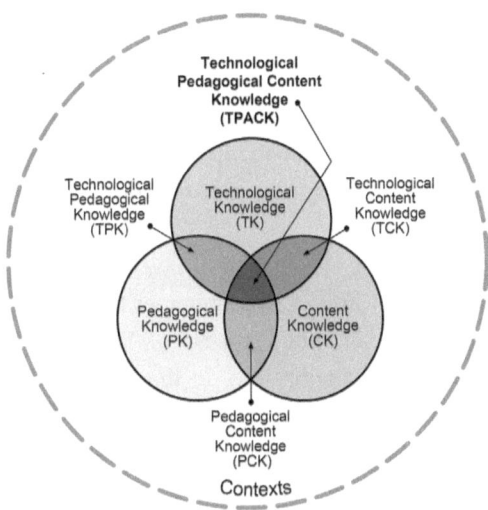

---

2. Reproduced with permission of the publisher, © 2012 by tpack.org; http://matt-koehler.com/tpack2/using-the-tpack-image/

Chapter 5

1.3. The SAMR model

Developed by Puentedura (2006), the SAMR model is intended to describe the levels of technology integration into teaching and learning: *substitution, augmentation, modification,* and *redefinition*. As illustrated in Figure 2, *substitution* refers to technology as a substitute without functional change; *augmentation*, as a substitute with functional change; *modification*, as a tool for redesigning tasks; and *redefinition*, as a tool for creating new tasks. For example, an online version of printed reading texts is an example of substitution; dictionary search embedded in the online reading texts is an example of augmentation; multimedia software used to annotate the online reading texts is an example of modification; mind-mapping software used to display the visual aspects of the reading texts is an example of redefinition. It is assumed that teachers use technology more effectively at the levels of modification or redefinition, as opposed to the levels of substitution or augmentation.

However, problems with differentiating the SAMR scale occur. Hamilton, Rosenberg, and Akcaoglu (2016) noted that the SAMR model did not take into account the context in which technology integration occurs. For example, they indicated that a computer supported investigation in a science class may be considered a case of transformed learning, but in practice such design is not feasible to ten students working on a single computer in a poverty-stricken school. The inclusion of contexts into the applications of the SAMR model could prevent researchers and teachers from over-generalising their prescriptions of technology integration.

In addition, Hamilton et al. (2016) also commented that the SAMR model views technology integration as a simplified process in which learning products rather than learning processes are emphasised. In this sense, they exemplified the way an English teacher requires his/her students to make their research reports using online presentation tools. This end product of technology integration may be deemed higher on the SAMR scale. However, the process of collecting literature and analysing data may not be enhanced with technology. Product over process would prevent researchers and teachers from understanding a whole picture of technology integration when they differentiate the SAMR scale.

Figure 2. Puentedura's (2006) SAMR model[3]

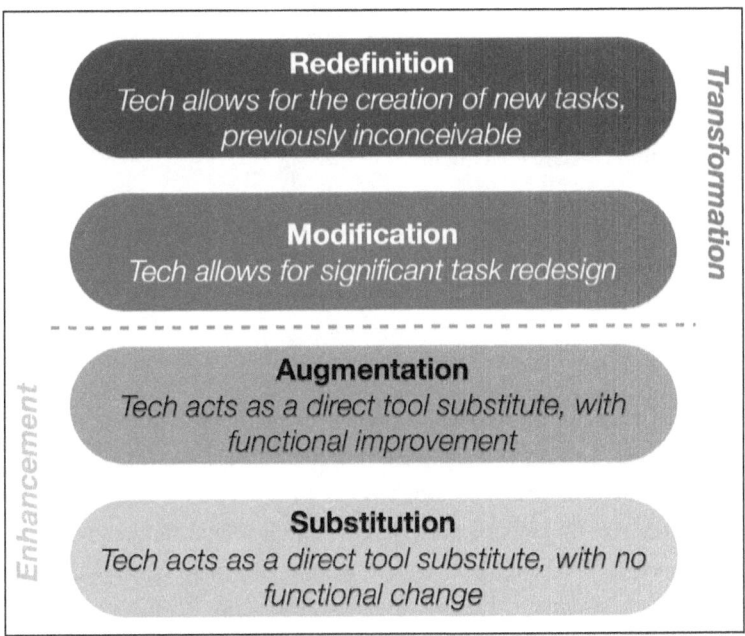

1.4. Research questions

Although the SAMR model is popular among practitioners, few empirical studies based on this framework have been conducted. Thus, there is a need to provide empirical evidence to ascertain the differentiation of the SAMR scale, with an emphasis on the process and product of technology integration as well as on the inclusion of contexts. To fill this gap, the present study adopted the SAMR model to investigate the degree to which four Taiwanese EFL teachers enacted their TPACK in the context of teaching English with iPads over the course of one school year. In addition, this study also intended to identify contextual factors

---
3. http://www.hippasus.com/rrpweblog/archives/2014/08/27/SAMRInTheClassroom.pdf

that might influence the levels of their TPACK enactments. Based on the above research rationales and purposes, the present study is guided by the following two questions:

- To what extent did the four EFL teachers enact their TPACK in relation to iPad-based English teaching?

- What were the contextual factors, if any, that might influence the levels of their TPACK enactments?

2. Method

2.1. Participants

Four EFL teachers in Taiwan were invited to participate in this study. Their pseudonyms were Nancy, Luke, Bellini, and Christine. Nancy, aged 45, had served as an elementary school teacher for 24 years; Luke, 38, as a high school teacher for 12 years; Bellini, 45, as a high school teacher for 21 years; and Christine, 43, as a high school teacher for 19 years. While Nancy, Luke, and Bellini had integrated iPads into English teaching from one semester to one school year, Christine did not have any experience in using the tablet in classroom teaching. The four teachers came from different schools in Taiwan.

2.2. Research setting

This research project was situated in the teachers' classrooms. These were equipped with a desktop computer (or a laptop computer), an LCD projector, a screen, and a wireless network. In addition, an Apple TV was installed to enable them to project their iPads onto the screen. As such, the teachers did not have to glue themselves to fixed desktop computers; instead they could circulate among students with their iPads at hand. This mobility allowed the teachers not only to display teaching materials from either the tablets or the desktop computers, but also to make close observations and give immediate feedback to students.

2.3. Research procedures

The whole research project spanned one school year. In order to help the participating teachers transform their teaching with iPads, the following procedures were operated:

- understanding the concepts of TPACK and SAMR: at the beginning of the research project, the teachers were introduced to the concepts of TPACK and SAMR. Particular emphasis was placed on how they examined their teaching using the two frameworks. More specifically, they were guided to analyse how subject-matter teaching was aligned with both iOS apps utilised and pedagogical methods employed. Afterwards, they moved on to explore and develop their understanding of how teaching could be transformed with mobile technology via the lens of the SAMR model;

- designing and implementing iPad-based instructions: with knowledge of TPACK and SAMR, the teachers learned to apply the two theoretical frameworks to teaching practices by creating iPad-based teaching materials and incorporating them into instructional activities and tasks. Such teaching ran for one school year; and

- sharing teaching through discussions: although the teachers possessed knowledge of TPACK and SAMR, it was not guaranteed that they had no difficulty in applying the theoretical concepts to teaching practices. To ensure this, they were encouraged to seek more inspirations in which bona fide examples associated with iPad-based teaching were demonstrated. For this reason, three Adobe Connect meetings were arranged respectively in the middle of the first semester, at the beginning of the second semester, and at the end of the second semester. While the professor (this author) illustrated anecdotes that depicted how the concepts of TPACK and SAMR were embodied in iPad-based English teaching, the teachers took turns and shared their experiences in applying iPads to their classroom teaching. Each of the three web-based conferencing meetings lasted for approximately two hours.

2.4. Data collection

Data regarding the levels of the teachers' TPACK enactments associated with their iPad-based teaching were collected through video recordings. Towards the end of the first semester, one 50-minute iPad-based teaching conducted by each of the four teachers was video-recorded. This procedure was repeated at the end of the second semester. Eight video recordings were utilised to assess the degree to which the teachers enacted their TPACK. Afterwards, the researcher conducted a focus-group interview with the four teachers, in order to clarify any implicit messages hidden in the videos, such as *What made you teach this way?*, *What were the teaching objectives you wanted to achieve?*, and *Were there any reasons for integrating this app into the teaching of vocabulary?*. The whole interview was audio-recorded and transcribed verbatim for data analysis.

Data regarding contextual factors were collected through three web-based conferencing sessions and one focus-group interview, as described above. The teachers shared ideas through Adobe Connect on different impediments to integrating iPads into their teaching. Finally, the researcher clarified and confirmed the contextual problems, if any, with the teachers in the focus-group interview.

2.5. Data analysis

To assess the degree of the teachers' TPACK enactments, the present study undertook quantitative content analysis: (1) determining video segments for analysis, (2) coding with an analysis framework, and (3) counting the occurrences of coding in particular categories (Riffe, Lacy, & Fico, 1998). First of all, teaching episodes involving the utilisation of apps were chosen since the app-enhanced teaching would indicate how the teachers applied their TPACK to iPad-based instructions. Then, the researcher coded the video segments using the SAMR model, with an emphasis on the process of how iPads were used in particular contexts. Each of the video segments was coded into a particular level of the SAMR model. Lastly, all of the codes in each level were counted. The counts indicated towards which SAMR level the teachers' iPad-based teaching was oriented. In addition, to illustrate the ways the teachers enhanced/ transformed their teaching, the TPACK framework was utilised to describe how the teachers incorporated the apps into the teaching of particular language knowledge and skills in a specific pedagogical manner.

To identify contextual factors that impacted on the teachers' TPACK enactments, qualitative data analysis procedures were undertaken: (1) coding, (2) developing categories, (3) comparing data, and (4) determining themes (Silverman, 2000). Special attention was paid to any technical and pedagogical problems about the integration of iPads into English teaching.

3. Results and discussion

3.1. The levels of TPACK enactments

The coded teaching episodes intended to measure the extent to which the teachers enacted their TPACK associated with their iPad-based teaching. As can be seen in Table 1, 19 teaching episodes were categorised under the level of substitution; 16 teaching episodes under the level of augmentation; five teaching episodes under the level of modification; and none of the teaching episodes under the level of redefinition. It is apparent that, while the teachers utilised iPads mostly to enhance their teaching (the number of enhancement episodes: 19+16=35), they also demonstrated their competencies in transforming teaching with iPads (the number of transformation episodes: 5+0=5).

Table 1. The levels of the teachers' TPACK enactments

Teachers	Semesters	Substitution	Augmentation	Modification	Redefinition
Nancy	1st	2	1	1	0
	2nd	1	1	2	0
Luke	1st	2	4	0	0
	2nd	3	4	0	0
Bellini	1st	4	0	0	0
	2nd	4	0	2	0

Chapter 5

Christine	1st	2	2	0	0
	2nd	1	4	0	0
Total		**19**	**16**	**5**	**0**

To illustrate how the levels of TPACK enactments were determined according to the SAMR model, the following are the descriptions of how the four teachers taught English using iPads at particular levels of the SAMR scale.

Luke used Popplet as a mind-mapping tool to help his students comprehend a reading article about animals' reactions towards earthquakes. With only one iPad device available to the teacher, Luke projected the process of creating a mind map together with students onto the screen in order to overcome the problem of students' lack of access to iPads. The teacher stated that Popplet-created mind maps were clearer and neater, compared to mind-map drawings on the blackboard. This instance of technology integration was rated the level of augmentation since the mind-mapping app substituted hand drawings with functional improvement.

Similarly, Christine used Popplet to visually present grammar: categorising prepositional phrases about travel transportations (e.g. by bus, by train, and by plane). She made the mind map viewable to students by projecting it onto the screen. This integration of Popplet into teaching grammar was an instance of augmentation.

In order to improve the restrictions imposed on textbook-based teaching, Nancy conducted a Bring Your Own Device (BYOD) project, in which students were encouraged to bring their iPads to class. Cooperating with an art teacher, Nancy guided students to produce iMovie videos that recorded their introductions to how they created pottery works. More specifically, the students produced their pots first, then shot photos of the pottery works with iPad cameras, filmed videos of interviews about their pottery creation with iPad cameras, and finally edited the material through iMovie. The case of recording students' pottery creations was deemed as an instance of modification in that iPads enabled the students to produce and annotate multimedia.

Inspired by Nancy's pottery creation project, Bellini organised an eco-traveller project, in which she and her students travelled to a tourist spot with their own iPads, with a purpose of shooting mini-films in which the students would introduce the attraction in English to future foreign visitors. The students worked in teams to collect information, take photos of sceneries, and film their narrations. Afterwards, they compiled materials and produced video clips through iMovie. In the end, they presented the outcomes of the mini-films. The use of iPads in this project was rated at the level of modification, like the way Nancy used iPads in her pottery creation project.

The levels of the four teachers' TPACK enactments were found mostly at the level of substitution and augmentation according to the SAMR model, albeit with a few teaching episodes reaching the level of modification. That is, iPads were predominantly utilised to enhance English teaching. A possible explanation for this result might be that iPads served as a substitute of transmitting linguistic knowledge to students in the context of conventional teacher-centred teaching. What is surprising is that using mind-mapping apps to present reading content and grammar in the present study was rated at the level of augmentation, contrary to Puentedura's (2006) redefinition example of using a mind map tool to visually represent structural aspects of texts. This discrepancy supports Hamilton et al.'s (2016) remark that the differentiation of SAMR should not ignore the process of technology integration. This finding has an important implication for teachers and teacher educators to understand the importance of technology integration processes in differentiating the levels of the SAMR scale.

3.2. Contextual factors

With regard to contextual factors that impacted on the teachers' TPACK enactments, three broad themes emerged from the analysis:

Access to mobile devices
"Due to the limited access to mobile devices, I once asked my students to bring their cell phones to the class for group activities and we did that. However, I just couldn't make this practice regular" (Luke).

"We just relied on the iPad owned by the teacher, with the majority of the students learning by watching. In order to increase the opportunity of learning with mobile devices among individual students, it is suggested that the Education Bureau accept iPad requests submitted by schools, in order for more students to benefit" (Christine).

Management of tablet computers
"Some students constantly chatted and romped. When they were free or when the teacher had not arrived, they were playing game apps" (Nancy).

"If the number of mobile devices increases in the classroom, many variables and unexpectations will occur. Sometimes managing these devices would make us feel frustrated, consume our time, and slow our curriculum progress" (Luke).

Access to wireless bandwidth
"The insufficiency of network bandwidth on campus made the teachers pay the cost of going online through the hotspots on their cell phones. How long would such enthusiasm continue?" (Bellini).

"iPads need to be connected to wireless network; unfortunately, the network connection on campus was not very stable" (Christine).

On the whole, these findings suggested that the teachers were concerned about technological access and support when they used iPads in classroom teaching. Their concern could be explained by the fact that the access to iPads and a wireless network was not sufficiently made available for the teachers and their students. It was very likely that this technological problem hindered the teachers' TPACK enactments towards the higher levels of the SAMR scale. Thus, students' access to mobile technology was critical in MALL. This finding was also reported by Aiyegbayo (2015) and Burston (2014, 2017). One of the issues that emerges from this finding is that policymakers can consider investing in building infrastructure of MALL, if MALL is to be implemented.

4. Conclusion

The purpose of this study was to investigate the degree to which the teachers enacted their TPACK in the context of iPad-based English teaching as well as identify contextual factors that might influence the levels of their TPACK enactments. The results of this investigation show that although some of the teachers' iPad-based teaching indicated their competency in transforming their teaching, their practice was predominantly enhanced by tablets as a substitute to deliver linguistic input to their students in conventional teacher-centred classrooms. In addition, students' access to iPads and a wireless network was considered essential in iPad-based English teaching. This technological problem might constrain the teachers from enacting TPACK towards the higher levels of the SAMR model.

The present study contributes to the literature on TPACK by providing empirical evidence on investigating the extent to which EFL teachers enacted their TPACK via the lens of the SAMR model. However, the small sample size did not allow the findings to be generalisable to all English teachers, so a further study could develop a questionnaire instrument to assess how other English teachers apply their TPACK to MALL from the perspective of SAMR. Moreover, this study was limited by the lack of students' access to iPads, so future studies can be conducted, ensuring that students can have access to them.

Acknowledgements

This work was supported by the Ministry of Science and Technology, Taiwan [grant number 102-2410-H-003 -037-].

References

Aiyegbayo, O. (2015). How and why academics do and do not use iPads for academic teaching? *British Journal of Educational Technology, 46*(6), 1324-1332.

Burston, J. (2014). MALL: the pedagogical challenges. *Computer Assisted Language Learning, 27*(4), 344-357. https://doi.org/10.1080/09588221.2014.914539

Burston, J. (2017). MALL: global prospects and local implementation. *CALL-EJ, 18*(1), 1-8.

Eubanks, J. F., Yeh, H. T., & Tseng, H. (2018). Learning Chinese through a twenty-first century writing workshop with the integration of mobile technology in a language immersion elementary school. *Computer Assisted Language Learning, 31*(4), 346-366. https://doi.org/10.1080/09588221.2017.1399911

Hamilton, E. R., Rosenberg, J. M., & Akcaoglu, M. (2016). The substitution augmentation modification redefinition (SAMR) model: a critical review and suggestions for its use. *TechTrends, 60*, 433-441. https://doi.org/10.1007/s11528-016-0091-y

Hao, Y. (2016). The development of pre-service teachers' knowledge: a contemplative approach. *Computers in Human Behavior, 60*, 155-164. https://doi.org/10.1016/j.chb.2016.02.054

Hsu, C. K. (2015). Learning motivation and adaptive video caption filtering for EFL learners using handheld devices. *ReCALL, 27*(1), 84-103. https://doi.org/10.1017/S0958344014000214

Hsu, L. (2016). Examining EFL teachers' technological pedagogical content knowledge and the adoption of mobile-assisted language learning: a partial least square approach. *Computer Assisted Language Learning, 29*(8), 1287-1297. https://doi.org/10.1080/09588221.2016.1278024

Hutchison, A., Beschorner, B., & Schmidt-Crawford, D. (2012). Exploring the use of the iPad for literacy learning. *The Reading Teacher, 66*(1), 15-23. https://doi.org/10.1002/TRTR.01090

Khodabandeh, F., Alian, J. E., & Soleimani, H. (2017). The effect of MALL-based tasks on EFL learners' grammar learning. *Teaching English with Technology, 17*(2), 29-41.

Koehler, M. J., Mishra, P., & Yahya, K. (2007). Tracing the development of teacher knowledge in a design seminar: integrating content, pedagogy and technology. *Computers & Education, 49*(3), 740-762. https://doi.org/10.1016/j.compedu.2005.11.012

Lin, C. C. (2014). Learning English reading in a mobile-assisted extensive reading program. *Computers and Education, 78*, 48-59. https://doi.org/10.1016/j.compedu.2014.05.004

Lin, C. C., & Yu, Y. C. (2017). Effects of presentation modes on mobile-assisted vocabulary learning and cognitive load. *Interactive Learning Environments, 25*(4), 528-542. https://doi.org/10.1080/10494820.2016.1155160

Mishra, P., & Koehler, M. J. (2006). Technological pedagogical content knowledge: a new framework for teacher knowledge. *Teachers College Record, 108*(6), 1017-1054. https://doi.org/10.1111/j.1467-9620.2006.00684.x

Niess, M. L. (2011). Investigating TPACK: knowledge growth in teaching with technology. *Journal of Educational Computing Research, 44*(3), 299-317. https://doi.org/10.2190/EC.44.3.c

Puentedura, R. (2006). *Transformation, technology, and education.* http://hippasus.com/resources/tte/

Riffe, D., Lacy, S., & Fico, F. (1998). *Analyzing media messages: quantitative content analysis.* Lawrence Erlbaum Associates.

Silverman, D. (2000). *Doing qualitative research: a practical handbook.* SAGE Publications.

Sun, Z., Lin, C. H., You, J., Shen, H. J., Qi, S., & Luo, L. (2017). Improving the English-speaking skills of young learners through mobile social networking. *Computer Assisted Language Learning, 30*(3-4), 304-324. https://doi.org/10.1080/09588221.2017.1308384

Young, K. (2016). Teachers' attitudes to using iPads or tablet computers: implications for developing new skills, pedagogies and school-provided support. *TechTrends, 60*(2), 183-189. https://doi.org/10.1007/s11528-016-0024-9

6 Personal learning environments and personal learning networks for language teachers' professional development

Cecilia Goria[1], Angelos Konstantinidis[2], Bryan Kilvinski[3], and Betul Eroglu Dogan[4]

Abstract

The emergence of Web 2.0 has created diverse opportunities for continuing professional development in the area of language teaching. This article begins by presenting how the pedagogical model implemented in an online postgraduate programme integrates the Personal Learning Environment and Personal Learning Network (PLE and PLN) concept and practice to support students' learning. Furthermore, it provides two case studies from the students of the programme on the integration of the PLE and PLN concept in their own settings as well as its effects on their professional development. The first case study describes how the PLE and PLN concept has become part of the instructional strategy of the teacher and discusses the outcomes of its implementation. The second case study deals with how the PLE and PLN concept facilitated the professional networking activities of the teacher and how this has affected teaching practices. The two case studies demonstrate diverse ways as to how teachers can use PLEs and PLNs for supporting their own as well as their students' learning, and for creating professional development opportunities within their

1. University of Nottingham, Nottingham, United Kingdom; cecilia.goria@nottingham.ac.uk

2. University of Nottingham, Nottingham, United Kingdom, Open University of Catalonia, Barcelona, Spain; angelos.konstantinidis@nottingham.ac.uk

3. University of Nottingham, Nottingham, United Kingdom, Mahidol University, Salaya, Thailand; bryan.kilvinski@gmail.com

4. Abdullah Tokur Primary School, Ankara, Turkey; 1ergl1btl@gmail.com

How to cite this chapter: Goria, C., Konstantinidis, A., Kilvinski, B., & Dogan. B. E. (2019). Personal learning environments and personal learning networks for language teachers' professional development. In C. N. Giannikas, E. Kakoulli Constantinou & S. Papadima-Sophocleous (Eds), *Professional development in CALL: a selection of papers* (pp. 87-99). Research-publishing.net. https://doi.org/10.14705/rpnet.2019.28.872

own teaching and educational contexts. The two case studies also demonstrate the potential of PLEs and PLNs for supporting teachers' professional development beyond a formal training programme.

Keywords: teacher professional development, personal learning environment, online postgraduate programme, case study.

1. Introduction

Rapid advancement of technologies and the emergence of Web 2.0 in the last decades have created new and diverse opportunities for continuing professional development in the area of language teaching.

This chapter focuses on the notion and practice of PLEs and PLNs and their impact on the experience of language teachers studying for a postgraduate professional development programme; the Master of Arts in Digital Technologies for Language Teaching (MA in DTLT), University of Nottingham, UK.

PLEs (Attwell, 2007) and PLNs (Drexler, 2010) are developing concepts which emerge from the idea that learning occurs in different online contexts due to ubiquitous computing and web 2.0 technologies. They emphasise the continuing character of learning and the central role of the individuals in taking responsibility and organising their own learning activities.

The educational context which hosts our present discussion not only acknowledges the importance of students' PLEs and PLNs for their learning and professional development, it also engulfs students' PLEs and PLNs in its pedagogical model (Goria & Konstantinidis, 2017; Konstantinidis & Goria, 2016).

This study addresses the ways in which the personalised learning supported by PLEs and PLNs affects the development of our students as learners as well as professionals.

After a brief review of the current literature around the notion of PLEs and PLNs, our chapter will demonstrate how it is introduced to the student-teachers of the MA in DTLT and promoted with practice throughout the duration of the programme.

Second, it will present and discuss two case studies from the students of the programme on the implementation of the PLE and PLN concept and its effects on their own professional development. In the first case study, it is described how the concept has become part of the instructional strategy of the teacher. The outcomes of its implementation are briefly discussed. The second case study deals with how PLEs and PLNs have facilitated the professional and pedagogical networking activities of the teacher and how they have affected the teaching practices. In both case studies, our students reflect on the impact of the notion and practice around PLEs and PLNs on their professional development as teachers.

The last section of the chapter places the outcomes of the case studies within the relevant literature and discusses the potential of PLEs and PLNs for supporting teachers in formal and informal learning as well as in professional development activities.

2. Method

2.1. Context

Our study is located within the context of the MA in DTLT; a two-year part-time distance learning programme that targets qualified teachers interested in developing their theoretical and practical expertise in digital technologies with a specific focus on the learning and teaching of foreign languages.

The programme's pedagogical model is articulated around principles of cognitive and experiential approaches to course design (Toohey, 1999), which consider social interaction and personal experience essential for constructing knowledge.

The result is a highly participatory pedagogical model which requires an equally highly engaged community within which our learners participate.

Konstantinidis and Goria (2016) advance a model for a community of distance learners which combines *teaching, social,* and *cognitive* presences of the Community of Inquiry (CoI) (Garrison, Anderson, & Archer, 1999) with *cohesion, identity,* and *creativity* of the Community Indicator Framework (CIF) (Galley, Conole, & Alevizou, 2014), respectively. Most significantly, the proposed model places CIF's *participation* at the centre of the learning experience[5].

In its original formulations, CoI is concerned with formal learning in closed learning communities, whereas CIF pertains to informal learning in open communities. Thus, the combination of these two frameworks is motivated by the drive to build a learning community that on the one hand is situated within the parameters of an institutionally based formal education programme, the MA in DTLT, and on the other hand, it operates on the basis of principles of open learning. With this in mind, PLEs and PLNs are promoted as an approach to prioritise open learning and nurture an open community of learners.

2.2. PLEs and PLNs and their integration in the programme

In our work, PLEs are the space within which learning takes place with all the resources utilised within that space. As for PLNs, they highlight the central role of personal and professional connections of the individual through social media, digital tools, and other communication media, including offline ones. Thus, PLEs provide the structure – space and technologies – for developing

---

[5]. To summarise, CoI proposes that learning happens at the intersection between teaching presence (the design and facilitation of the educational experience), cognitive presence (the extent that participants are in position to construct meaning through communication), and social presence (participants' ability to project their socioemotional traits into the community). CIF identifies the four ingredients of an affective community learning experience, namely: "participation (the ways in which individuals engage in activity), cohesion (the ties between individuals and the community as a whole), identity (how individuals perceive the community and their place within it), and creative capability (the ability of the community to create shared artefacts and knowledge)" (Galley et al., 2014, p. 379).

people's PLNs and communities (Steeples & Jones, 2002 as cited in Drexler, 2010, p. 370). Through PLEs and PLNs, our programme promotes an approach to learning that "is not about individuals as much as it is about networks, sharing, and creating" (Laakkonen, 2011, p. 24).

Furthermore, PLEs and PLNs meet the needs of professionals as they bring together different types of learning; typically informal learning, formal learning, professional learning, and learning from the home (Attwell, 2007). They provide personalised working spaces that enable "multidirectional learning in which the students can use all the available resources and people on the internet" (Pérez Cascante, Salinas, & Marín, 2016, p. 54).

Within the MA in DTLT, PLEs and PLNs are introduced in phases in line with the three-level framework proposed by Dabbagh and Kitsantas (2012). Phase 1 focusses on personal productivity; in Phase 2, the learners transform their learning spaces from personal to social; in Phase 3, the learners reflect on the outcomes of the previous phases and customise them around their own learning goals. An additional Phase 4, the 'go public' phase (Goria & Konstantinidis, 2017), is introduced for the learners to develop their spaces from social to globally social. Throughout all phases, the learners reflect on and graphically represent their spaces and connections, they categorise their tools and connections according to their purpose and functions, and position and reposition themselves inside their spaces as users as well as contributors.

Through our PLE and PLN based approach, our community of learners is extended beyond the boundaries of our programme to include our learners' professional and personal experiences. In a participatory-pedagogy fashion (Andersen & Ponti, 2014; Siemens, 2008), knowledge constructed outside our programme is brought into the programme via our learners' PLEs and PLNs, affecting the overall learning experience.

In the next section, we outline some outcomes of our implementation of this approach.

3. Results

A desired outcome of our practice around PLEs and PLNs briefly outlined above is increased awareness of the services, tools, and connections that support learning and of their influence on our students' experience directly (Goria & Konstantinidis, 2017) as well as indirectly on their students' experience (Goria, 2016). In the following two sections, two case studies are presented, as evidence of the impact of our PLE and PLN approach on two of our learners' professional practices.

3.1. Case study of integration of PLEs in instruction

In the section below, one of our students and co-author of this chapter reports on his methods for integrating the PLE concept in teaching. He discusses how the integration transformed his practice and created new opportunities for professional development.

3.1.1. Case study context

Our student has an information technology background and works as a computer-assisted language learning instructor at the Faculty of Information and Communications Technology (ICT) at Mahidol University, Thailand. His students study for the completion of a degree in ICT, have high technological skills, and their English language level ranges from lower intermediate to advanced. The number of students in his classes is usually between twenty and thirty. As part of this degree in ICT, he teaches 18-week modules which mainly focus on reading and writing skills.

3.1.2. Description of the instructional methods

The PLE concept is introduced from the first week of each course that he teaches. He starts the course by posing the simple question: *What is an environment?*, to ensure that students understand the meaning of the word 'environment' and to prepare the class for the following activities. The class collectively produces definitions for an environment, a learning environment, and a PLE. He then pairs the students randomly and asks them to list the things around them that help them learn. Students usually start reporting very basic tools, such as books, pens, and so on, but soon they mention more sophisticated tools and technologies, such as computer devices, the internet, websites, applications, and social networks.

Next, students are tasked with drawing their PLE as a diagram, taking a photo of their PLE with their mobile phones and sharing their work using a class instant messaging group. The photos are then shared on a screen while different aspects of the PLEs are discussed within the class, focussing on the features that people have in common and those that are unique to some PLEs. In this way, the students are supported in visualising their own PLE and gradually guided to become aware of the instruments that they use.

The teacher also asks students to add aspects of their PLEs into a shared online mind map, as a further exercise to be completed outside of the classroom and to help students learn from each other and develop their own PLE over the duration of the course. The content of a PLE varies from student to student, reflecting the individual differences in language learners. Facebook, Wikipedia, and specific YouTube channels related to course content or English grammar appear regularly, and online grammar checking and plagiarism detection tools are common, as well as more specialised online computer programming and developing communities such as Github and StackOverflow.

3.1.3. *How the integration of the PLEs impacted upon the teaching process*

The courses relevant to this study are taught by four instructors who observe and reflect upon how the PLEs are developed and interpreted by the students, leading to implementing changes to the PLE assignment and concept each time the syllabus is reviewed. Notes, which form the basis of observations and reflections, are made by the instructors to a shared Google Docs. The integration of the PLEs brought several favourable changes into the overall teaching process. Compared to previous deliveries of the course, the students were given more autonomy in their learning; for example, they became more meticulous with their assignments and were more likely to use proofreading tools or other resources to check their work rather than rely on their instructors.

The utilisation of the PLE by students also facilitated the peer review process and collaboration between the students. It could be argued that the PLEs enabled the students to visualise and use the tools and people around them, whilst also developing their own independence. What is more, due to the introduction of the PLEs, the types and aims of assessment were transformed and became more authentic and relevant to the students. Whilst previous exam questions had been graded to a specific standard of grammar, the new assignment tasks required students to reflect on their use of their own PLE or describe how they might use aspects of it to support the writing process and create their own language learning environment based on their own experiences and interests.

3.1.4. The impact on professional development as a teacher

Besides directly impacting the teaching process and the role of the teacher, the PLE concept had several profound effects on the teacher's professional development.

Before being introduced to the concept of the PLE, he had his own favourite tools, methods, and strategies for learning. By becoming cognisant of the concept and by giving it a formal name, he was able to make it part of his teaching practice, and as a result his teaching practice improved. By helping his students construct their own PLE, he further improved his relationship with each student and this enabled him to become familiar with their different interests and approaches to learning. Moreover, through the process of PLE development that he introduced, he learned from his students as he became aware of a number of new learning resources, websites, and applications. On a more personal level and as a language learner himself, he viewed the development of a PLE as the most effective way of learning a new language and achieving proficiency. Lastly, he noticed that the successful outcomes of his practice motivated his colleagues to adopt PLEs in their own lesson.

Cecilia Goria, Angelos Konstantinidis, Bryan Kilvinski, and Betul Eroglu Dogan

3.2. Case study of use of online communities as part of the PLN

In the following paragraphs, another student of the MA in DTLT and co-author in this paper reports on how developing her PLN to include online teaching communities has helped her find information and elaborate ideas relevant to her daily teaching, expand her professional network, find potential partners for developing pedagogical projects, enrich her teaching practices, and hone her teaching skills. Her PLE/PLN experience as learner of the programme has helped her develop competencies that have transformed her professional practice.

3.2.1. Case study context

Our student is an English language teacher in a primary school in Ankara, Turkey. After embracing the notion and practice of PLEs and PLNs as a student of the MA in DTLT, she has been regularly using online social and professional networks such as eTwinning, Facebook, and EBA, a network for teachers and students in Turkey, for searching information, staying up-to-date, finding partners for pedagogical projects, and taking part in discussions about educational issues.

She currently utilises each of the aforementioned three online communities in different ways in order to achieve her goals and meet her needs as a teacher. She monitors daily nearly twenty Facebook groups related to education and language learning and accesses EBA twice a week to explore the affordances of the platform, search resources, watch other teachers' videos about their curriculum practices, as well as read the comments and discussions related to these videos.

In sharp contrast with Facebook and EBA, she uses eTwinning only as a tool to find partners for developing exchange projects. She enters the eTwinning platform frequently at the beginning of the school season to search for potential partners or to join existing projects. However, past the initial search for partners, she logs into the platform only occasionally and mainly for administrative purposes, news and updates.

3.2.2. *The impact on professional development as a teacher*

By including these three online communities into her PLN, she is able to enrich her daily teaching in a number of ways and create opportunities for professional development. Her claim is that, through her PLN, she finds lesson plans that have been tested and recommended by other teachers in the field and reads about the challenges that might emerge on implementation and how more experienced teachers address these challenges. This, as she claims, eases the implementation process by decreasing the effort and time needed to organise classroom activities.

The PLE and PLN practice has provided her with the opportunity to expand her professional network, communicate with teachers across Europe interested in developing telecollaborative projects, and become partner in a few telecollaborative projects. Her experience helped her to apply a practical understanding of the theoretical knowledge that she gained through her participation in the MA in DTLT programme on a variety of issues related to organising telecollaborative projects, such as partner selection, partner-to-partner communication and rapport building, overcoming problems, caring for students' personal needs, devising engaging and effective activities. What is more, her involvement in the design and development of telecollaborative projects helped her strengthen her ICT, communication, and project management skills, while she also became more proficient in creating a stimulating environment for project-based learning for her students.

4. Discussion

The two case studies demonstrate ways in which teachers can use PLEs/PLNs for supporting their own and their students' learning, as well as for creating professional development opportunities within their own teaching and educational contexts. In agreement with the literature concerned with PLEs and PLNs, our case studies describe how these are used for: accessing resources suitable for the specific needs of the user (Pérez Cascante et al., 2016); increasing students' motivation (Dabbagh, Kitsantas, Freih, & Fake, 2015); searching, aggregating, creating, and sharing content (Saadatmand & Kumpulainen, 2013); encouraging students to make their learning personally relevant; increasing students' collaboration and independence (Castañeda & Soto, 2010); assisting students in reflecting on the learning process (Arrufat & Sánchez, 2012); and engaging in online communities (Saadatmand & Kumpulainen, 2013).

However, what differentiates our two case studies is that they describe how the PLE and PLN concept has been employed by teachers as a medium for professional development beyond the formal education programme with which they were involved. This demonstrated how the PLE and PLN concept realises its true potential for supporting lifelong learning and continuous professional development (Attwell, 2007). By suggesting a new way of understanding and using digital technologies and social media for learning, the PLE and PLN concept recognises the role of the individuals in organising their own learning, it corroborates the continuity character of learning, and seeks to provide the tools and methods for supporting such learning. PLEs and PLNs can equally support teachers who want to enhance their daily teaching practices, expand their professional network, or create their own professional development opportunities. Moreover, the PLE and PLN concept also recognises that learning occurs in diverse contexts and is not attributable to a single educational source. As such, PLEs and PLNs support learning both within and beyond formal education.

5. Conclusions

In this chapter, we have presented how the pedagogical model implemented within the MA in DTLT programme introduces our students to the concept and practice of PLEs and PLNs. Two case studies have been reported to demonstrate the impact of our model on the professional development of our students in their own educational settings. The case studies show the potential of PLEs and PLNs for supporting teachers both in their daily practice and in creating their own professional development opportunities beyond a formal training programme. Future research will explore the methods for language teachers to extend students' utilisation of PLEs and PLNs beyond classroom instructions, aiming at strengthening the sustainability and transferability of the practice.

References

Andersen, R., & Ponti, M. (2014). Participatory pedagogy in an open educational course: challenges and opportunities. *Distance Education*, *35*(2), 234-249. https://doi.org/10.10 80/01587919.2014.917703

Arrufat, M. J. G., & Sánchez, V. G. (2012). Steps to reflect on the personal learning environment. Improving the learning process? In *PLE Conference Proceedings* (Vol. 1). http://revistas.ua.pt/index.php/ple/article/download/1430/1316

Attwell, G. (2007). Personal learning environments – the future of elearning? *ELearning Papers*, *2*(1), 1-8.

Castañeda, L., & Soto, J. (2010). Building personal learning environments by using and mixing ICT tools in a professional way. *Digital Education Review*, *18*, 9-25.

Dabbagh, N., & Kitsantas, A. (2012). Personal learning environments, social media, and self-regulated learning: a natural formula for connecting formal and informal learning. *The Internet and Higher Education*, *15*(1), 3-8. https://doi.org/10.1016/j.iheduc.2011.06.002

Dabbagh, N., Kitsantas, A., Freih, M. A., & Fake, H. (2015). Using social media to develop personal learning environments and self-regulated learning skills: a case study. *International Journal of Social Media and Interactive Learning Environments*, *3*(3), 163-183. https://doi.org/10.1504/IJSMILE.2015.072300

Drexler, W. (2010). The networked student model for construction of personal learning environments: balancing teacher control and student autonomy. *Australasian Journal of Educational Technology*, *26*(3), 369-385. https://doi.org/10.14742/ajet.1081

Galley, R., Conole, G., & Alevizou, P. (2014). Community indicators: a framework for observing and supporting community activity on Cloudworks. *Interactive Learning Environments*, *22*(3), 373-395. https://doi.org/10.1080/10494820.2012.680965

Garrison, D. R., Anderson, T., & Archer, W. (1999). Critical inquiry in a text-based environment: computer conferencing in higher education. *The Internet and Higher Education*, *2*(2-3), 87-105. https://doi.org/10.1016/S1096-7516(00)00016-6

Goria, C. (2016). *From innovative teachers to innovative learners*. Presented at the Inside Government - Raising the standards of Modern Languages Education, Manchester.

Goria, C., & Konstantinidis, A. (2017). *Implementing openness in a private online course: theory, practice, and reflections*. Presented at the EUROCALL 2017 – CALL in a climate of change: adapting to turbulent global conditions, Southampton, UK.

Konstantinidis, A., & Goria, C. (2016). Cultivating a community of learners in a distance learning postgraduate course for language professionals. In S. Papadima-Sophocleous, L. Bradley & S. Thouësny (Eds), *CALL communities and culture – short papers from EUROCALL 2016* (pp. 230-236). Research-publishing.net. https://doi.org/10.14705/rpnet.2016.eurocall2016.567

Laakkonen, I. (2011). Personal learning environments in higher education language courses: an informal and learner-centred approach. In S. Thouësny & L. Bradley (Eds), *Second language teaching and learning with technology: views of emergent researchers* (pp. 9-28). Research-publishing.net. https://doi.org/10.14705/rpnet.2011.000004

Pérez Cascante, L., Salinas, J., & Marín, V. (2016). Use of an institutional personal learning environment to support learning actions in higher education. *AtoZ: Novas Práticas Em Informação e Conhecimento, 5*(1), 53-63. https://doi.org/10.5380/atoz.v5i1.46937

Saadatmand, M., & Kumpulainen, K. (2013). Content aggregation and knowledge sharing in a personal learning environment: serendipity in open online networks. *International Journal of Emerging Technologies in Learning (IJET), 8*(S1). https://doi.org/10.3991/ijet.v8iS1.2362

Siemens, G. (2008). *New structures and spaces of learning: the systemic impact of connective knowledge, connectivism, and networked learning*. http://www.elearnspace.org/Articles/systemic_impact.htm

Steeples, C., & Jones, C. R. (2002). *Networked learning: perspectives and issues* (2nd ed.). Springer Verlag.

Toohey, S. (1999). *Designing courses for higher education*. Open University Press.

7 Assessing the efficacy of VR for foreign language learning using multimodal learning analytics

Tom Gorham[1], Sam Jubaed[2], Tannishtha Sanyal[3], and Emma L. Starr[4]

Abstract

This chapter describes a small-scale pilot study in which participants in the experimental group learned how to write Japanese kanji characters within an immersive Virtual Reality (VR) graffiti simulator (the Kingspray Graffiti Simulator on the Oculus Rift VR system). In comparing the experimental group to the non-VR control group in the context of embodied cognition, the authors used a multimodal learning analytics approach: the participants' body movements were recorded using a full-body 3D motion-tracker and clustered with a machine learning algorithm. The participants were also compared on the basis of a written posttest and a follow-up survey.

Keywords: computer assisted language learning, virtual reality, machine learning, multimodal learning analytics, Japanese writing.

---

1. Harvard Graduate School of Education, Cambridge, United States; tsg181@mail.harvard.edu

2. Harvard Graduate School of Education, Cambridge, United States; saj229@mail.harvard.edu

3. Harvard Graduate School of Education, Cambridge, United States; tas651@mail.harvard.edu

4. Harvard Graduate School of Education, Cambridge, United States; ems519@mail.harvard.edu

How to cite this chapter: Gorham, T., Jubaed, S., Sanyal, T., & Starr, E. L. (2019). Assessing the efficacy of VR for foreign language learning using multimodal learning analytics. In C. N. Giannikas, E. Kakoulli Constantinou & S. Papadima-Sophocleous (Eds), *Professional development in CALL: a selection of papers* (pp. 101-116). Research-publishing.net. https://doi.org/10.14705/rpnet.2019.28.873

Chapter 7

1. Introduction

1.1. Language learning, VR, and embodied cognition

Around the world there is encouragement for students to learn a foreign language (Devlin, 2015; Jackson, 2013). There is good reason for this; in addition to the potential economic and social benefits of being bilingual, there is evidence that it can also improve executive functions in children – a suite of cognitive skills that are strong predictors of future success, which include inhibition, working memory, and cognitive flexibility (Bialystok, 2015). Unfortunately, learning a foreign language can be an arduous and occasionally frustrating experience for many students (Lightbown & Spada, 2013). One of the underlying reasons for the current study is to examine one potential avenue that could make this process more effective, efficient, and enjoyable.

The present study examines one facet of foreign language learning: writing in a foreign script, particularly in one that is significantly different to a student's mother language. More specifically, it investigates the possible affordances that a fully immersive VR environment may offer for facilitating this process. For this study, a VR graffiti simulator was chosen as a comparison to traditional pen and paper approaches to foreign language writing practice. The novel VR experience might increase the participants' interest and enjoyment and hence improve their motivation and attitude (Lightbown & Spada, 2013). There is evidence that students who take handwritten notes of class lectures have better recollection and understanding of the material compared to students who type their notes using their laptops (Mueller & Oppenheimer, 2014). This may be due to the relatively slower speed of handwriting or it may result from the different patterns of brain activation that are caused by the fine motor manipulation of the pen (Kiefer et al., 2015). At any rate, to date, there has been little to no research done in making a comparison between foreign language writing practice done with pen and paper and similar practice done in an immersive VR environment.

It is worthwhile to research the educational affordances of VR because of the phenomenon of embodied cognition. It is the strong reciprocal relationship between the body and the mind, wherein the "perceptual and motor systems influence the way we construct concepts, make inferences, and use language" (Repetto, Serino, Macedonia, & Riva, 2016, para. 3). VR has the potential to leverage this embodied cognition to help improve the language learning outcomes of students (Macedonia, Müller, & Friederici, 2011; Repetto, Cipresso, & Riva, 2015). Because of this, an immersive virtual graffiti simulator might offer some benefits over more traditional approaches. For example, the students practise writing the scripts on extremely large canvases that appear to the user to be several meters in length and height. In order to 'paint' the characters in appropriately large fonts, they must use their entire bodies, reaching high, and squatting down low. However, measuring the physical interaction with the VR technology poses some significant challenges for data collection. To address these challenges, we turned to multimodal learning analytics and machine learning.

1.2. Multimodal learning analytics

Blikstein and Worsley (2016) consider multimodal learning analytics to be a central issue in the long-running educational battle between behaviourism (or neo-behaviourism) and constructivism. When it comes to measuring outcomes, they assert that the behaviourist side has traditionally had the advantage. That is because it relies on relatively easier approaches to data collection, including psychometrics and standardised testing, compared to the ones employed by researchers who study constructivist approaches. Blikstein and Worsley (2016) point out that many educators have spent decades calling for constructivist methodologies that are student-centred and focus on student autonomy – including such luminaries as Dewey, Freire, Montessori, and Barron and Darling-Hammond. However, the widespread adoption of such methodologies has been hampered by the challenge of data collection for research.

Fortunately, advances in hardware and machine learning may hold the promise of making constructivist approaches considerably easier to evaluate. Schneider and Blikstein's (2014) research progressed with the use of the Microsoft Kinect™ – a sensor that uses infrared light for full-body 3D motion capture and simple facial recognition – to investigate the correlation between changes in body posture during a learning activity and learning outcomes. Also, eye-tracking technology and computer vision machine learning algorithms were used to explore the pedagogical implications of joint visual attention (see Schneider & Blikstein, 2014; Schneider & Pea, 2013, 2014; Schneider et al., 2015). The outcomes of this chapter are closely connected to the aforementioned studies.

The present study was conducted as a graduate student research project overseen by Schneider. We took particular inspiration from one of his studies mentioned in the previous paragraph (Schneider & Blikstein, 2014). In that study, the researchers collected approximately 1 million data points regarding the X, Y, and Z cartesian coordinates of their test subjects' body movements using the Kinect™. To make sense of this huge amount of data, the researchers utilised an unsupervised machine learning algorithm called K-means. The K-means algorithm does not sort data into predefined categories (that would be called supervised machine learning); instead, it clusters data into novel groupings (see Bahnsen & Villegas, 2017 for an accessible introduction to K-means clustering). Through this clustering, the researchers were able to identify three prototypical body positions: active, semi-active, and passive. They were then able to draw correlations between the subjects' posture and the learning outcomes (e.g. surprisingly, there was a positive correlation between the number of transitions between active and passive positions and better learning outcomes).

We employed a similar approach in the present study. We collected 3D motion capture data with the Kinect™ sensor, clustered the data using the K-means algorithm, and attempted to identify prototypical body positions that might correlate to learning gains.

2. Method

2.1. Hypotheses

Some assumptions underlie the hypotheses of this study. First, language teachers can improve their students' motivation and attitude by providing activities that are enjoyable and interesting, which may in turn improve learning outcomes (Lightbown & Spada, 2013). Second, increased physical movement in the context of embodied cognition will result in improved learning outcomes (Kiefer et al., 2015; Repetto et al., 2016). Third, learners will exhibit greater body movements (the head and arms specifically) when using VR to learn a new script versus pen and paper. Based on these assumptions, we developed two hypotheses for this study:

- Learners will exhibit greater excitement and engagement using VR to learn a new script versus pen and paper.

- Learners who use VR are able to reproduce the script characters more accurately as compared to those who learned using pen and paper.

We hoped to find some indication of prototypical body positions that might correlate to learning gains.

2.2. Participants

The participants for this study were three female students in their 20's at the Harvard University Graduate School of Education. We used convenience sampling to recruit the participants for this study; participants were people that the researchers knew and informally recruited. Because of the demographic makeup of the school, it was easier to recruit female participants. Participants had no previous experience using VR and no previous experience with the Japanese kanji script. All of the participants were native English speakers from the United States of America. Participants were not compensated for participation. Two participants (labeled as VR001 and VR002) were assigned to the experimental group that received the VR treatment. The third participant (labeled as VR003) was assigned to the control group which studied using traditional pen and paper.

2.3. Materials and data collection tools

We tested all participants on their ability to remember and write the seven basic logograms for the days of the week written in the Japanese kanji script as well as their English transliteration (e.g. 月 = 'getsu'=Monday; 火 = 'ka'=Tuesday; 水 = 'sui'=Wednesday; etc.).

The participant (VR003) in the control group was given a paper-based list of the seven target Japanese Kanji characters which included their stroke order and their English transliteration. She was also given a desk, a blank notebook, and a pen to use for studying.

The participants (VR001 and VR002) in the experimental group took part in the study individually. Each person used an Oculus Rift VR system which was running on an Alienware X51 personal computer and playing the VR app, Kingspray Graffiti Simulator (Figure 1). Within the virtual environment, a list of the seven target Japanese kanji characters which included their stroke order and their English transliteration was pre-painted on the graffiti wall. To get a better sense of what the experience of painting in the Kingspray Graffiti Simulator is like, we recommend that readers watch a short demonstration video (https://youtu.be/dhIxY6G-UHE).

All participants' sessions were video recorded with a smartphone to facilitate behavioural observations. Participant's motions during the session were tracked using a Microsoft Kinect™ (Figure 1) using a data collection tool developed by Dr Bertrand Schneider (which can be found at https://github.com/hgse-schneider/Kinect_Data_Collection_Tool). This data was then analysed and clustered using the K-means machine learning algorithm within the data visualisation software, Tableau. Although the data collection tool records information about multiple body parts, including the X, Y, and Z cartesian coordinates of the participant's hands, wrists, elbows, shoulders, and spine, for the purposes of this chapter, we will focus on the analysis and clustering of the X and Y coordinates of the participants' heads.

After the alloted length of study time, all participants took a paper-based posttest to assess their ability to remember and correctly reproduce the kanji logograms for the days of the week and the phonetic spelling of each symbol in English. After that, each participant filled out an online survey to assess their engagement in the learning activity. The follow-up survey included 28 Likert scale evaluations of statements that covered engagement-related topics such as novelty, aesthetics, involvement, and endurability.

Figure 1. Set-up of the experimental VR condition (**Left**: The Oculus Rift sensor in the foreground and the KinectTM sensor in front of the monitor; **Right**: A participant (background) squatting down while using the Oculus Rift and the KinectTM software (foreground) recording her movement on a laptop)

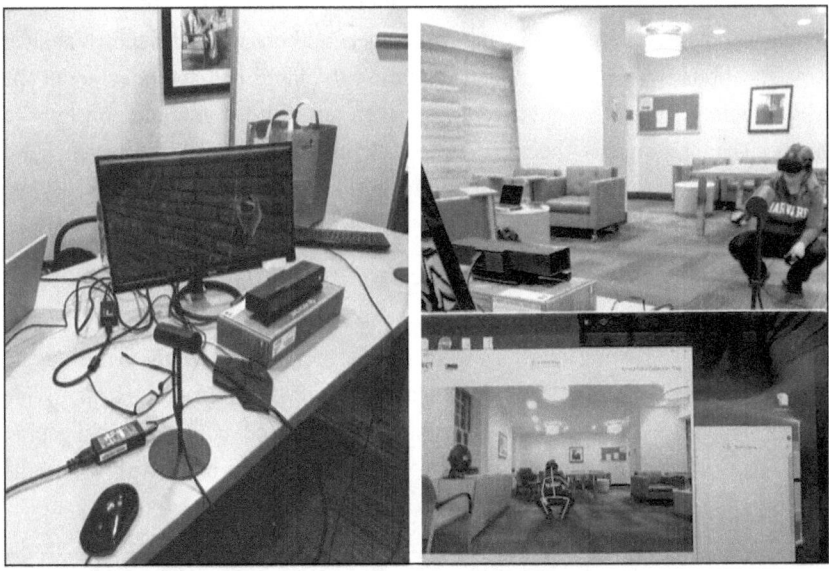

2.4. Procedure

The participant (VR003) in the control group was given a paper-based list of the seven target Japanese Kanji characters which included their stroke order and their English transliteration. She was also given a desk, a blank notebook, and a pen to use for studying. One of the researchers/authors was on hand to answer any questions she had regarding character shape, stroke order, or English transliteration. The participant was not given any further guidance on how to study. The participant then had up to 20 minutes to study the seven kanji characters. After the study period, the participant took the paper-based posttest and then filled out the online learning engagement survey.

The participants (VR001 and VR002) in the experimental group received the treatment separately. Each participant was first set up in the Oculus Rift VR headset by the researchers and led through a five- to ten-minute tutorial on how to navigate and interact with the VR environment. After this tutorial, on a wall in the virtual environment the participants could see a pre-painted list of the seven target Japanese Kanji characters, including their stroke order and their English transliteration. One of the researchers/authors was on hand to answer any questions the participants had regarding the kanji characters or about the VR system. The participants were not given any further guidance on how to study. The participants then had up to 20 minutes to study the seven kanji characters within the VR graffiti simulator (Figure 2). After the study period, each participant took the paper-based posttest and then filled out the online learning engagement survey.

Figure 2. The participants' view in experimental condition while using the Oculus Rift and Kingspray Graffiti Simulator[5] (**Left**: Wide 'screenshot' of the alley environment used within the Kingspray simulator; **Right**: Close-up 'screenshot' of the brick wall where the participants practiced their kanji characters)

---

5. Reproduced with kind permissions from Kingspray.

3. Results

3.1. Descriptive statistics

The participant (VR003) in the control condition performed better than the participants (VR001 and VR002) in the experimental condition, with a posttest score of 19 (out of 21) compared to the VR001's score of 7 and VR002's score of 12. However, the VR participants reported higher engagement in the online follow-up survey than the control participant, with VR001 rating the activity as 1.19 on a scale of -2 to 2, VR002 rating it a 1.67, and VR003 rating it 0.98.

In addition to the posttests and the online follow-up survey, all of the participants' sessions were video recorded with a smartphone to facilitate behavioural observations (Table 1). The experimental group expressed more interest and excitement than the control did, but it also expressed more discomfort and asked more questions. As an example of an expression of excitement, experimental group participant, VR002, exclaimed, "Ok! This is so fun!".

Table 1. Behavioural observations from videos of participants' sessions and results from posttests and follow-up surveys

	VR001 (experimental)	VR002 (experimental)	VR003 (control)
Number of times verbally expressing interest in activity	2	1	0
Number of times verbally expressing excitement	3	9	0
Number of times verbally expressing discomfort	2	2	1
Number of times participant asks experimenter a question	8	4	1
Paper-based posttest results (out of 21 points)	7	12	19
Online follow-up survey measuring engagement (on a scale from -2 to 2	1.19	1.67	0.98

Chapter 7

3.2. Clusters

As mentioned earlier, because we were inspired by the phenomenon of embodied cognition and Schneider and Blikstein's (2014) research, we hoped to find some indication of prototypical body positions that might correlate to learning gains. To do this we used a Microsoft Kinect™ (Figure 1) data collection tool to gather three-dimensional body movements and position data. We chose the X and Y cartesian coordinates of the participants' heads to serve as a simple proxy for physical movement and position. We then clustered that data using a K-means unsupervised algorithm in the Tableau data visualisation software. This clustering performed in Tableau resulted in three clusters: high, medium, and low (Figure 3).

Figure 3. Head X and head Y clusters (Tableau)

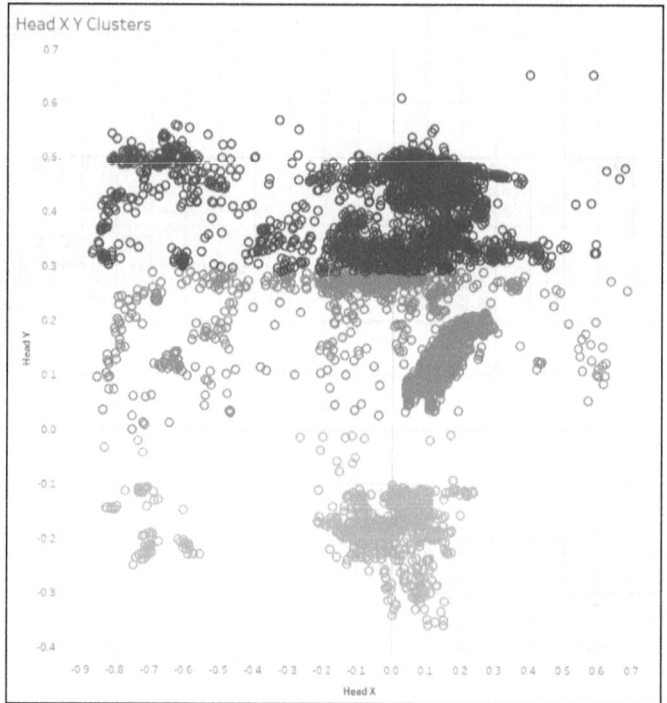

In the high cluster, participants had high head Y values, demonstrating that they were standing upright or even reaching up. In the medium cluster, participants were leaning over, producing lower head Y values. In the low cluster, participants had extremely low head Y values, which were indicative of crouching or squatting. See Table 2 for examples of what each prototypical body posture looks like.

Table 2. Head X and head Y cluster prototypical postures

High Cluster	Medium Cluster	Low Cluster

Figure 4. Timelines of clusters of relative head position based on head X and head Y values, by participant

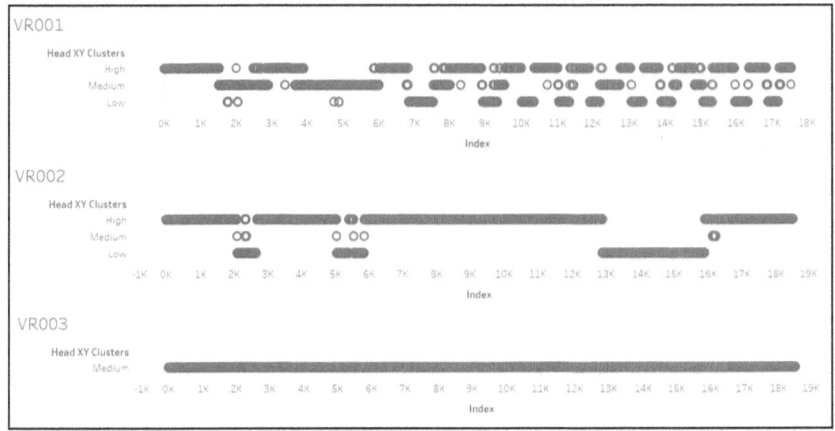

Figure 4 shows the times that each participant was in one of these three clusters. Note that because the data collection tool was recording data points 15 times

per second for approximately 20 minutes, the timeline shown in the X axis in Figure 4 runs to 18,000 (15 data collection points per second times 60 seconds times 20 minutes equals 18,000). This shows that the participant in the control group (VR003), who was sitting down at a desk working in a notebook, stayed exclusively in the medium cluster. In comparing the participants in the experimental group, VR001 switched frequently between all of the clusters, whereas VR002 spent most of her time in the high cluster and less frequent, but relatively longer times in the low cluster.

4. Discussion

Our first hypothesis was that participants in the experimental group would exhibit greater excitement and engagement using VR to learn a new script versus pen and paper. Based on the results of the current study, this was found to be true. This is not particularly surprising because the Kingspray Graffiti Simulator is designed as a commercial off-the-shelf VR video game, and its primary purpose is to entertain and engage its users. Furthermore, the participants had no prior experience with VR, so as a novel experience, it was likely to be more exciting than traditional pen and paper study.

Our second hypothesis was that participants in the experimental group would be able to remember and reproduce the kanji characters more accurately as compared to the participant in the control group. However, the posttest contradicted this hypothesis. The control participant achieved a much higher posttest score than either of the VR participants.

These unexpected results have many possible explanations. First, it is possible that the medium of the test might have played a role in the outcome. Namely, the posttest was administered as a written paper test. The control participant practised in the same medium as the test was administered in, while the VR treatment group did all of their practice within an immersive digital environment which was considerably different than the medium in which they were tested. It is possible that this raises issues of transfer. Perhaps in future iterations of this study, the posttest could be administered in the virtual environment for both groups to see if the testing medium has an effect on learning outcomes.

A second explanation is that the novel VR environment itself hindered the learning of the VR treatment group. This could either be attributed to a steeper learning curve (and thus increased cognitive load) involved in becoming acclimated to the VR control scheme or possibly because the digital environment contains many distractions. For instance, the virtual alleyway in which the participants practised featured realistic elements like birds and passing trains which might have drawn the participants' attention away from the target task.

The findings of this study suggest one particularly interesting route for future investigation. Because the control participant utilised well-known study techniques such as spaced repetition but the participants in the VR condition reported higher engagement, perhaps it would be valuable to test a new experimental condition in which both the paper and VR approaches were combined.

In this proposed future study, participants would begin by practising on paper using established and proven techniques (like spaced repetition) for a period of time. Then, once they feel comfortable with the material that they were studying, they would then enter the VR environment for a shorter period of time. Within the digital environment, the participants would be asked to make a large-scale, artistic visualisation of the characters that they had been studying.

This approach would address challenges which might arise when using VR in second language learning. It leverages the best elements of both treatment approaches; the participants get high-quality and high-volume practice on paper, supplemented by the novel and engaging experience of the VR treatment. There is also a practical benefit to this mixed approach. VR equipment is currently expensive, so it would be unlikely that most classrooms would have enough equipment for each student to have their own headset. In the mixed approach, the students would do the majority of their practice on paper and only a short amount (i.e. five or ten minutes) within the VR environment. This would be a more feasible approach for classrooms with limited access to VR technology.

One final point that is worth considering for future VR and multimodal learning analytics research is that the better performing participant in the experimental group (VR002) had a movement pattern that was more similar to the control participant (VR003); she had long periods of less movement and fewer transitions between clusters (Figure 4). It is possible that this is an indication of increased concentration and focus during practice. More research is needed to determine if this pattern of movement does, in fact, correlate with improved learning outcomes.

5. Conclusions

This pilot study introduces a possible way that multimodal learning analytics can supplement an evaluation of a language learning intervention using VR. Although the results of the study did not support the hypothesis that participants studying Japanese kanji with VR would outperform a participant using a more traditional method, it suggests ways in which this line of inquiry can be expanded. Larger sample sizes and the mixed approach (VR plus pen and paper) described in the previous section are both promising avenues for future research.

Acknowledgements

We would like to thank our professor, Bertrand Schneider, and our teaching assistants, Joseph Reilly and Jeffrey King, for their support throughout this study.

References

Bahnsen, A. C., & Villegas, S. (2017). *Machine learning algorithms explained – K-means clustering*. https://blog.easysol.net/machine-learning-algorithms-3/

Bialystok, E. (2015). Bilingualism and the development of executive function: the role of attention. *Child Development Perspectives, 9*(2), 117-121.

Blikstein, P., & Worsley, M. (2016). Multimodal learning analytics and education data mining: using computational technologies to measure complex learning tasks. *Journal of Learning Analytics, 3*(2), 220-238. https://doi.org/10.18608/jla.2016.32.11

Devlin, K. (2015). *Learning a foreign language a 'must' in Europe, not so in America.* http://www.pewresearch.org/fact-tank/2015/07/13/learning-a-foreign-language-a-must-in-europe-not-so-in-america/

Jackson, A. (2013). *Foreign language policies around the world.* http://blogs.edweek.org/edweek/global_learning/2013/03/foreign_language_policies_around_the_world.html

Kiefer, M., Schuler, S., Mayer, C., Trumpp, N. M., Hille, K., & Sachse, S. (2015). Handwriting or typewriting? The influence of pen- or keyboard-based writing training on reading and writing performance in preschool children. *Advances in cognitive psychology, 11*(4), 136-46.

Lightbown, P. M., & Spada, N. (2013). *How languages are learned* (4th ed.). Oxford University Press.

Macedonia, M., Müller, K., & Friederici, A. D. (2011). The impact of iconic gestures on foreign language word learning and its neural substrate. *Human Brain Mapping, 32*(6), 982-998. https://doi.org/10.1002/hbm.21084

Mueller, P. A., & Oppenheimer, D. M. (2014). The pen is mightier than the keyboard. *Psychological Science, 25*(6), 1159-1168. https://doi.org/10.1177/0956797614524581

Repetto, C., Cipresso, P., & Riva, G. (2015). Virtual action and real action have different impacts on comprehension of concrete verbs. *Frontiers in Psychology, 6*, 1-9. https://doi.org/10.3389/fpsyg.2015.00176

Repetto, C., Serino, S., Macedonia, M., & Riva, G. (2016). Virtual reality as an embodied tool to enhance episodic memory in elderly. *Frontiers in Psychology, 7*, 1-4. https://doi.org/10.3389/fpsyg.2016.01839

Schneider, B., & Blikstein, P. (2014). Unraveling students' interaction around a tangible interface using gesture recognition. In J. Stamper, Z. Pardos, M. Mavrikis & B. Mclauren (Eds), *Proceedings of the 7th International Conference on Educational Data Mining (EDM'14)* (pp.320-323). http://educationaldatamining.org/EDM2014/proceedings/EDM2014Proceedings.pdf

Schneider, B., & Pea, R. (2013). Real-time mutual gaze perception enhances collaborative learning and collaboration quality. *International Journal of Computer-Supported Collaborative Learning, 8*(4), 375-397. https://doi.org/10.1007/s11412-013-9181-4

Chapter 7

Schneider, B., & Pea, R. (2014). Toward collaboration sensing. *International Journal of Computer-Supported Collaborative learning,* 9(4), 371-395. https://doi.org/10.1007/s11412-014-9202-y

Schneider, B., Sharma, K., Cuendet, S., Zufferey, G., Dillenbourg, P., & Pea, A. D. (2015). 3D tangibles facilitate joint visual attention in dyads. In O. Lindwall, P. Hakkinen, T. Koschmann, P. Tschounikine & S. Ludvigsen (Eds), *Proceedings of the International Conference on Computer Supported Collaborative Learning 2015: Exploring the Material Conditions of Learning (CSCL'15)* (Vol.1, pp. 158-165). The International Society of the Learning Sciences.

8. Interpreting technologically fluent classrooms: digital natives' attitudes towards the use of technology in primary schools in Norway

Georgios Neokleous[1]

Abstract

This qualitative study provides baseline data on young learner attitudes towards the use of technology in primary schools. Through individual interviews, the students highlighted the importance of its application and acknowledged its potential in the education process. The benefits that they put forward are grouped into four categories: technology-infused classrooms promote (1) collaboration, (2) active learning, (3) authenticity, and (4) higher order thinking skills. The findings also reveal a general favourable consensus among the interviewees regarding their teachers' efforts to adopt technology in class. Yet, students cautioned that technology-integrated lessons should fulfil specific classroom purposes while stressing at the same time the importance of satisfactory preparation before their implementation. For the students, the use of technology should essentially serve two purposes: (1) provide an engaging and interactive alternative to the traditional approach to teaching, and (2) address different learning styles. Acknowledging the student voice, the study concludes, contributes effectively to the optimisation of the learning experience.

Keywords: digital natives, digital literacy, 21st century classroom, student voice.

---

1. Norwegian University of Science and Technology, Trondheim, Norway; georgios.neokleous@ntnu.no

How to cite this chapter: Neokleous, G. (2019). Interpreting technologically fluent classrooms: digital natives' attitudes towards the use of technology in primary schools in Norway. In C. N. Giannikas, E. Kakoulli Constantinou & S. Papadima-Sophocleous (Eds), *Professional development in CALL: a selection of papers* (pp. 117-129). Research-publishing.net. https://doi.org/10.14705/rpnet.2019.28.874

Chapter 8

1. Introduction

Literacy has customarily been linked to the linguistic and functional ability to read and write. Recently, however, there has been a gradual shift away from this perception to a more advanced and multivalent definition that introduces new literacies that do not simply focus on reading and writing (Krulatz & Neokleous, 2018; Lankshear & Knobel, 2011). The multivalence of literacy is already mirrored in various national curricula including, for instance, Australia and Norway (ACARA, 2016; Norwegian Directorate for Education and Training, 2016), with digital literacy being highlighted as quintessential in 21st century education (Lankshear & Knobel, 2011). In fact, the Norwegian national curriculum has identified digital literacy as the fifth basic skill in every subject at every level and an important prerequisite for schooling along with reading, writing, arithmetic, and oral fluency (Norwegian Directorate for Education and Training, 2016). Because of the emphasis on digital competence, most schools across Europe have been equipped with the latest forms of digital tools and infrastructure to enhance young learners' technological aptitude and fluency (Almås & Krumsvik, 2007). Despite the importance placed on digital competence, research revealed that primary school teachers interpreted this newly acquired focus in varied ways and, consequently, in many cases had different expectations from their students (Engen, Giæver, & Mifsud, 2015). In trying to unearth the reasons behind the discrepancy as to what digital competence in young learners should entail, through collecting data by educators, researchers identified the inadequate formal education in teacher-training programmes (Engen et al., 2015).

While most studies regarding the use of technology in primary classrooms delved deeper into in- but also pre-service teacher attitudes (e.g. Petko, 2012), the lack of the student voice in research widens the gap that prevents bridging theory and classroom practice (Geer & Sweeney, 2012). A study, therefore, which would exclusively focus on primary school student attitudes through self-reporting, would give a more accurate portrayal as to what being technologically fluent in a digital age encompasses. At the same time, it would shed light on the pedagogical expectations young learners have from their teachers, and the constructs that support their learning in the 21st century classroom.

2. Method

Before proceeding with a discussion of the results, this section presents an overview of the research design that was adopted. Trying to elicit the views of primary-school students in Norway through interviews and classroom observations, the purpose of this chapter is to address the following questions:

- What do young learners think of the general presence, but also their teachers' use of technology in their classrooms?

- What is the value of using technology as a resource for learning as seen by the participants?

- For what purposes do participants believe technology should be used in the classroom?

Based on the list of questions, the most appropriate way to address them was by carrying out a qualitative study. Four 10th grade classes from four public schools situated in four different locations across Norway represented the sample. The rationale behind this decision was the depiction of a representative portrayal of the participants' perspectives. Collecting data from students in geographically different parts of a country is believed to generate a broader and a more varied portrayal of the results (Saldaña, 2015). In addition, the four teachers were selected as they all identified themselves as technology-enthusiasts who made frequent use of various forms of digital tools in the classroom (e.g. Chromebooks, web 2.0 tools). The four classes were observed during four different phases of an entire semester. The teachers agreed that on those dates their lessons would be technologically-enhanced. At the end of the semester, 14 students from these classes volunteered to be individually interviewed with an average of 3.5 students per class. Field notes taken during the observations encompassed the third data collection technique. Interview and observation protocols were also developed to assist the researcher in acquiring and preserving the study's focus during the data collection process.

The semi-structured interviews with the 14 students were transcribed and coded based on Saldaña's (2015) two coding cycle methods. The purpose was to ascertain the students' attitudes as far as the use of technology was concerned, but also to detect whether they agreed with their teachers' decisions concerning its integration in the classroom. The observational protocol rubrics and the field notes were also coded to further contribute to the triangulation of the results. The decision to carry out classroom observations and interviews with young learners required certain procedures pertaining to ethical considerations, including seeking approval from the Norwegian Centre for Research Data. Permission was granted from the administration of the four schools. Furthermore, the students' parents were informed about the presence of an observer in the classroom and the rationale behind this. Consent was also granted from the parents whose children were going to be interviewed. To ensure that the results of the observations would not have been altered and conditioned by disclosing to the participants the purpose of the study, the participants were made aware of the actual focus during the interviews. They were then asked whether they were still willing to take part. None of them wanted to withdraw.

3. Results and discussion

Overall, the 14 interviewees unanimously expressed their appreciation for the use of technology in the classroom. As they elaborated, integrating technology is "a requirement" in today's classrooms and a practice that "all schools should promote". The student-participants underlined its potential but also its value in all subject areas while they also emphasised its impact on classroom dynamics. Based on their learning experiences with technology in their classrooms, as exemplified in the following section, the advantages that they put forward in their interviews are grouped into four categories.

3.1. Student verdict on technology

3.1.1. Technology and collaboration

A specific aspect of technology-integrated lessons that the students highly valued was the opportunity they provided in helping them interact with their classmates in a way that traditional lessons do not. As Student 9 claimed: "Because I had the chance to work with my friends was something I liked". As Student 3 exemplified: "I enjoyed working with two of the guys in my class as we realised that we had so much in common, so I actually cannot wait to work with them again". Four of the young learners who defined themselves as "very shy" deemed the dynamic interaction opportunities that these lessons offered "helpful". Being asked by their teachers to cooperate in groups, as the four interviewees explained, made them actively participate while normally they would "sit back and just observe".

The four students of the second school cited the project collaboration with a classroom in a different part of the country through synchronous communication platforms and discussion boards as a "motivating experience" that encouraged "more engagement". In fact, what the students particularly enjoyed about the collaborative nature of technology-enhanced lessons was the positive classroom atmosphere cultivated along with the possibility of connecting and building links among them even outside the classroom. As they further elaborated, the learning environment boosted their self-confidence because it prompted them not to "be afraid to participate" as they were able to express themselves "without fear or judgment". Similarly, research studies have highlighted that technology can enhance collaborative learning (Yau et al., 2003).

3.1.2. Technology and active learning

Securing a more active role in the lesson was an additional benefit that the use of technology offered. During one of those lessons, as five students outlined: "It was one of the few times where we actually have to do something in class and not just listen to our teacher and, you know, copy stuff from the blackboard". In this way, they continued, "as each one of us was assigned, like, a role... learning is more fun". As opposed to the traditional teacher-fronted classroom, the technology-integrated lesson directly engaged students in the learning process as they had a leading role towards unfolding the intended learning objectives. As a result, this engagement fosters independence and cultivates a sense of responsibility to students. Active learning prompts them to take on responsibilities because for similar activities they do not have to rely on their teacher to accomplish a specific goal.

In their interviews, 11 students underlined that the possibility to contribute collectively to the completion of an activity rendered them more determined to reach the intended goal while it also sustained their motivation. Most significantly, as the 11 students elaborated, technology enabled them to actively interact and engage with the material being relayed based on their preferred learning styles. For instance, because it was effectuated in a way that was relevant to her needs, Student 7, who described herself as a visual learner, appreciated the use of concept-mapping web tools as it helped her structure her understanding and incorporate the new information into practice. The effectiveness of technology in promoting active learning, and thus enhancing learning outcomes, was also underlined in the literature (Shieh, 2012).

3.1.3. Technology and authenticity

In addition, ten students stated that the use of some of the technology tools in the classroom enabled them to focus on topics, issues, and materials that are of particular interest to them. In one of the four classrooms observed, the students had to listen to a Podcast excerpt that offered practical considerations of an abstract concept they were taught in class, and which triggered their interest. They then had to create their own Podcast in which they would explain to their classmates an abstract concept of their own choice with real-life examples. Student 2, who participated in this activity, described the tasks associated with specific technology tools, such as podcasts, as "more relevant, more useful than some of those of my textbook". As the excerpt illustrates, the students did not only endorse the authenticity of the audio-text because of its links with their interests and the outside world but also the authenticity of the task that followed because they "could take this and do it at home". Creating authentic learning situations has been one of the goals of classrooms across the world, as it is believed to enhance learning (Lever-Duffy, McDonald, & Mizell, 2002). The forty-eight pre-service teachers in Luo, Murray, and Crompton's (2017) recent study employed technology to create authentic learning opportunities. The findings showed that students displayed "a high level of engagement in reflective and collaborative learning" (Luo et al., 2017, p. 141).

3.1.4. Technology and higher order thinking skills

The ability of some of the technology tools used in their lessons to harness their creativity constituted for the students another important gain. For instance, as four interviewees exemplified, being able to create their own comic strip to display the different interpretations of the modal verb *can* in their English class made them understand that "there are fun and creative ways of practising English", without necessarily, Student 14 continued, being "a pharmacist or a waiter [in a role play]". Along with cultivating their creative skills, twelve students have also underlined technology's capacity to foster higher-order thinking, including decision-making and critical thinking skills. In one of their classes, students had to choose the best option between two different routes in a journey-mapping tool and justify their choice. Such tasks, as transpired from the student interviews, "make... [us] understand that we have to think through the decisions we make... and how difficult it is to make the best decision". Research findings have also shown that the integration of technology-enriched classroom settings enhances technology and higher order thinking skills (Hopson, Simms, & Knezek, 2001).

3.2. Student verdict on teacher use of technology

As outlined in the section above, several studies showed that technology-enhanced lessons have a positive impact on learning. Yet, the teacher's role is also pivotal in establishing a technology-integrated classroom that would promote learning with motivated and engaged students (Lever-Duffy et al., 2002). In this study, there was a general favourable consensus among the 14 interviewees regarding their teachers' efforts to employ technology. As it emerged, however, because the participants are competent users of technology themselves, they had heightened expectations that, as six students stated, "had not been delivered". For this reason, in their interviews, the students cautioned that technology-integrated lessons should fulfil specific purposes while they also stressed the importance of adequate teacher preparation before their implementation in class.

Ten students underlined the importance of technology accomplishing clearly defined objectives. Even though its integration in the classroom can act as a strong incentive, when there is a vague sense of direction from the teacher, Student 9 exemplified, "the lesson can get more interesting... but only for a while... I then drift away". This sentiment is echoed in the interviews with the students from the different schools as they stated that "most teachers think that just by using technology the lesson would be more interesting". For them, as they clarified, the different forms of technology the teacher introduces should have a clear purpose and should not be used just for the sake of it. As an example, Student 2 cited the lesson in which they were asked by their teacher to use their laptops to write the answers of a gap-fill task that was featured in their coursebook. Similar uses of technology, the participant argued, "cannot make the lesson more fun or more... captivating". Elaborating on this idea further, Student 1 continued, "it is not like this [activity] will make me learn cool stuff about Microsoft [Word]... it was perhaps easier for the teacher to collect the answers". This idea was also mirrored in Gorder's (2008) study, which revealed that essentially teachers used technology to facilitate the lesson and not to instil learning. The emphasis placed on how to work the digital tool shies students away from delving deeper into the learning opportunities and potentials that it offers (Bauer & Kenton, 2005; Wepner, Tao, & Ziomek, 2006).

In their interviews, students also stated that technology-integrated lessons often resulted in "wasting" classroom time to address technical issues that their teachers were in most cases "unaware how to fix". Their teachers' desire to employ various novice technological applications and tools in the classroom was criticised by seven students who argued that "we often spend time trying to teach our teacher how each [tool] works". As the interviewees elaborated, "it's like they want to impress us with trendy web tool without fully understanding what each tool can do". Not only do teachers not possess the required technical skills to carry out a task with certain forms of technology, Student 11 continued, "they sometimes do not pick it up fast, time is lost, and we don't even use technology in action". Literature also identifies the issue of inadequate teacher preparation pertaining to more complex technological tools (Ertmer, 2005; Gorder, 2008), with Gorder (2008) underlining that "teachers often learn along with the students" (p. 63).

3.3. Student verdict on purposes of technology in education

In fact, research studies underline the difference between mere technology integration and technology integration for learning (Bauer & Kenton, 2005; Gorder, 2008). Despite not seeing the true purpose of employing specific technology tools in the classroom, as outlined in the section above, the interviewees acknowledged that for the majority of them, there was a rationale behind their integration in their lessons. The appreciation and enthusiasm of venturing into activities that relied on the use of technology was unanimous with the students identifying it as a great incentive. Based on the interviews, the use of technology should essentially serve two purposes in the classroom: (1) provide an engaging and interactive alternative to the traditional approach to teaching, and (2) address students' different learning styles.

Through technology, ten interviewees underlined the move away from the traditional teacher-fronted classroom to a setting in which students assume creative control over their learning experience. For instance, as they elaborated, providing a platform to collaborate on group projects and presentations with students in different physical settings fostered more engaging and interactive classroom environments. This experience, they continued, which was not "restricted to searching on Google and jotting down notes", allowed for a dynamic interaction that enabled them to take responsibility of their learning "beyond the four walls of the classroom". As they articulated, "technology should encourage more… attractive instruction… It is through this attractiveness that we learn things". Increasing and sustaining students' motivation in the classroom has been a perennial pressing issue with which most teachers still grapple in their classrooms (Linnenbrink & Pintrich, 2003). Research has shown that technology and web tools act as motivators that can strengthen the students' want to learn (Liu, Hsieh, Cho, & Schallert, 2006). More recently, a study conducted by Granito and Chernobilsky (2012) through a period of nine weeks revealed the positive results that the use of technology can have on students' motivation to learn and retain new teaching material.

In addition to the alternative teaching paths that they offered, six students identified that one of the purposes of technology-enhanced lessons should be their capability of addressing different learning styles. The use of mind-mapping tools in one of the lessons, such as bubbl.us, provided visual learners with the opportunity to better process the information their teacher attempted to convey. In her interview, Student 7, who often complained that there are not enough visuals used, recognised her teacher's efforts to present new information in the form of graphics. Technology, however, as she explained, enabled her teacher to incorporate graphs and imagery in a way that helped her "organise the content of the lesson… and then apply what we learned in a new activity". As it readily transpires from the example the student offered, technology that is used with a clear purpose can assist the teacher in meeting the educational objectives, and thus enhance learning (Lever-Duffy et al., 2002).

4. Conclusions

Undisputedly, the prominence placed by national curricula on digital skills and competence is transparent across the world (Lankshear & Knobel, 2011). Teachers are encouraged to use devices such as smart boards and tablets to meet the students' needs and to facilitate learning. Most significantly, however, an important change that the integration of technology initiated is the gradual shift away from teacher-centred to student-centred classrooms with the students assuming control over their learning (Shieh, 2012). As the results of this study indicate, students acknowledged this change of focus and pinpointed it in their interviews as one of the greatest benefits of technology-infused lessons.

When designing such lessons, therefore, to generate a positive classroom impact and deeper learning opportunities, teachers should take into consideration certain key elements. Principally, it is important that the use technology has a clear sense of purpose with specific objectives in mind. Furthermore, the choice of digital tools should be accompanied by a focus on triggering motivation among students.

To guide teachers through a smooth integration of technology, primary schools could assign technology coaches. Their role would be that of a mentor who would assist in (1) familiarising in-service teachers with the latest digital tools and technological trends, but also (2) making sure that both the instructors and the students benefit from their use in the classroom. In addition, because of the pre-eminence of national curricula on digital competence as an important prerequisite and as primary school children are technologically fluent, teacher education programmes should also adequately train pre-service teachers in how to effectively employ technology in the classroom. Teacher trainers along with pre-and in-service teachers must understand the impact of technology in our contemporary society and promote, facilitate, and model fruitful digital learning experiences for students.

Despite the limited number of participants, the study paves the way for future research. Further research should explore in greater depth student perceptions on where and when young learners deem specific classroom-based technologies meet their needs and could contribute towards enhancing learning. Acknowledging the student voice would enable future research to centre on fields in which student and teacher views differ. Student-centred studies would effectively contribute to the optimisation of the learning experience and the fostering of a setting where digital natives will share the same language with their teachers.

References

ACARA. (2016). *Australian curriculum, assessment and reporting authority.* http://www.australiancurriculum.edu.au/

Almås, A. G., & Krumsvik, R. (2007). Digitally literate teachers in leading edge schools in Norway. *Journal of In-Service Education, 33*(4), 479-497. https://doi.org/10.1080/13674580701687864

Bauer, J., & Kenton, J. (2005). Toward technology integration in the schools: why it isn't happening. *Journal of technology and teacher education, 13*(4), 519-546.

Engen, B. K., Giæver, T. H., & Mifsud, L. (2015). Guidelines and regulations for teaching digital competence in schools and teacher education: a weak link? *Nordic Journal of Digital Literacy, 10*(2), 69-83.

Ertmer, P. A. (2005). Teacher pedagogical beliefs: the final frontier in our quest for technology integration? *Educational technology research and development, 53*(4), 25-39. https://doi.org/10.1007/BF02504683

Geer, R., & Sweeney, T. A. (2012). Students' voices about learning with technology. *Journal of Social Sciences, 8*(2), 294-303. https://doi.org/10.3844/jssp.2012.294.303

Gorder, L. M. (2008). A study of teacher perceptions of instructional technology integration in the classroom. *The Journal of Research in Business Education, 50*(2), 63-76.

Granito, M., & Chernobilsky, E. (2012). The effect of technology on a student's motivation and knowledge retention. *NERA Conference Proceedings, 17*. https://opencommons.uconn.edu/nera_2012/17

Hopson, M. H., Simms, R. L., & Knezek, G. A. (2001). Using a technology-enriched environment to improve higher-order thinking skills. *Journal of Research on Technology in education, 34*(2), 109-119. https://doi.org/10.1080/15391523.2001.10782338

Krulatz, A., & Neokleous, G. (2018). Fostering literacy in adolescent EFL classrooms: an overview of techniques and teaching ideas. *The European Journal of Applied Linguistics and TEFL, 7*(1), 57-72.

Lankshear, C., & Knobel, M. (2011). *New literacies*. McGraw-Hill Education.

Lever-Duffy, J., McDonald, J., & Mizell, A. (2002). *The 21st-century classroom: teaching and learning with technology*. Addison-Wesley Longman Publishing.

Linnenbrink, E. A., & Pintrich, P. R. (2003). The role of self-efficacy beliefs in student engagement and learning in the classroom. *Reading & Writing Quarterly, 19*(2), 119-137. https://doi.org/10.1080/10573560308223

Liu, M., Hsieh, P., Cho, Y., & Schallert, D. L. (2006). Middle school students' self-efficacy, attitudes, and achievement in a computer-enhanced problem-based learning environment. *Journal of Interactive Learning Research, 17*(3), 225-242.

Luo, T., Murray, A., & Crompton, H. (2017). Designing authentic learning activities to train pre-service teachers about teaching online. *The International Review of Research in Open and Distributed Learning, 18*(7), 141-157. https://doi.org/10.19173/irrodl.v18i7.3037

Norwegian Directorate for Education and Training. (2016). National curriculum. https://sokeresultat.udir.no/finn-lareplan.html#/&english?r3=%C7%82%C7%82456e67656c736b&r3val=Engelsk

Petko, D. (2012). Teachers' pedagogical beliefs and their use of digital media in classrooms: sharpening the focus of the 'will, skill, tool' model and integrating teachers' constructivist orientations. *Computers & Education, 58*(4), 1351-1359. https://doi.org/10.1016/j.compedu.2011.12.013

Saldaña, J. (2015). *The coding manual for qualitative researchers* (3rd ed.). Sage.

Shieh, R. S. (2012). The impact of technology-enabled active learning (TEAL) implementation on student learning and teachers' teaching in a high school context. *Computers & Education, 59*(2), 206-214. https://doi.org/10.1016/j.compedu.2012.01.016

Wepner, S. B., Tao, L., & Ziomek, N. M. (2006). Broadening our view about technology integration: three literacy educators' perspectives. *Reading Horizons, 46*(3), 215-237.

Yau, S. S., Gupta, S. K., Karim, F., Ahamed, S. I., Wang, Y., & Wang, B. (2003). Smart classroom: enhancing collaborative learning using pervasive computing technology. In *Proceedings of 2nd ASEE International Colloquium on Engineering Education (ASEE2003)* (pp. 1-10).

9. Materials design in CALL: a case study of two teachers of English as creators of digital materials

Ferit Kılıçkaya[1]

Abstract

The importance of providing pre-service and in-service teachers with sufficient training and practice in integrating technology into their classrooms has led several studies to investigate the possible effects of pre-determined training and practice provided to teachers. However, most of these studies seem to have focussed on teachers' beliefs and perceptions during the courses offered in the departments without considering their needs and requests. Noticing this gap, the current study aimed to investigate two in-service language teachers' views and experiences on the training which was designed and provided based on their needs and requests. This research was designed as a qualitative case study, focussing on the experience of two male teachers of English who were exposed to a series of workshops that focussed on creating digital materials using several web-based tools. The findings of the study indicated that, although the participants learned how to utilise the technological tools and were willing to infuse these tools into classrooms, their intentions, in some cases, were not realised in their classroom practices for various reasons, most of which were directly related to the context of teaching.

Keywords: materials design, CALL, English teachers, creating digital materials.

1. Burdur Mehmet Akif Ersoy University, Burdur, Turkey; ferit.kilickaya@gmail.com

How to cite this chapter: Kılıçkaya, F. (2019). Materials design in CALL: a case study of two teachers of English as creators of digital materials . In C. N. Giannikas, E. Kakoulli Constantinou & S. Papadima-Sophocleous (Eds), *Professional development in CALL: a selection of papers* (pp. 131-144). Research-publishing.net. https://doi.org/10.14705/rpnet.2019.28.875

© 2019 Ferit Kılıçkaya (CC BY)

Chapter 9

1. Introduction

As a response to opportunities provided by new technological developments, language teachers are eager to benefit from these new developments in their classrooms to support their students (e.g. Egbert, Paulus, & Nakamichi, 2002; Göktürk Sağlam & Sert, 2012). However, teachers familiar with the basic uses of technology, such as word-processing and publishing comments on blogs, sometimes find it difficult to create digital materials using the tools available on the Internet. Several factors affect the teachers' attitudes, as well as their practices regarding their uses of Computer Assisted Language Learning (CALL), such as lack of training in addition to lack of support provided by their institution (e.g. Aslan & Zhu, 2015; Garrett, 2009; Kessler & Plakans, 2008; Merç, 2015). Moreover, as indicated by Bates (2015), CALL benefits should enable teachers to deal with their workload. In other words, creating digital materials or using CALL applications should not require much time, and it could lead them to produce useful materials and to contribute to high-quality teaching.

Teacher education programmes play an important role in enabling teachers to better infuse technology into their classrooms as they can be provided with enough theoretical knowledge and practice. Without providing efficient training, equipping schools with computers and an Internet connection, in addition to other devices, and expecting teachers to use technology to improve their students' performance will result in failure and disappointment (Garrett, 2009; Son, 2018). Noticing the importance of providing necessary training and practice, several studies investigated the effects of providing training to language teachers (e.g. Egbert et al., 2002; Kılıçkaya & Seferoğlu, 2013), their perceptions and attitudes (e.g. Akayoğlu, 2017; Aslan & Zhu, 2015; Göktürk Sağlam & Sert, 2012), and preferences (e.g. Akayoğlu & Cirit, 2017; Merç, 2015; Uzun, 2016).

The study conducted by Egbert et al. (2002), for example, investigated how English as a second language and foreign language teachers used CALL activities after completing the graduate-level CALL course. The findings revealed that, when provided with training, teachers were more eager to benefit from CALL activities. The findings also indicated that for training and supporting teachers, the contexts and schools where teachers work should be considered. Another study conducted by Kılıçkaya and Seferoğlu (2013) aimed at determining the effects of CALL training on in-service language teachers' use of CALL-based activities. The findings indicated that the training on use of computer technologies which provided a link between second language theories and language learning principles led the participants to better infuse CALL materials into their classrooms. However, it was also noted that knowing how to use a computer or a tool did not result in its use in the language classroom.

Regarding language teachers' perceptions and attitudes, Göktürk Sağlam and Sert's (2012) study revealed that, despite the challenges and difficulties involved in integrating technology into their classrooms, in-service language teachers viewed technology-enhanced language learning and teaching positively and tried to benefit from technology in various ways in their classrooms. Similarly, Aslan and Zhu (2015) revealed the teachers' positive perceptions, although several participants expressed that they felt anxious regarding technology usage due to several issues, such as difficulty in learning the tools. Investigating the perceptions of 69 pre-service teachers of English towards an introductory CALL course at a state university in Turkey, Akayoğlu (2017) indicated that, although the participants were anxious about the course in the beginning, after the training the participants began to feel more confident about this course and suggested taking this course in the earlier stages of their programme.

Merç (2015), on the other hand, investigated pre-service language teachers' use of technology in their practice at schools during the last year of their programme and found that the participants complained about the lack of technology tools available in the schools. Moreover, there was a mismatch between the training provided in teacher training programmes and the real conditions in the classrooms as to technology integration. Similarly, Uzun (2016) underscored this mismatch by indicating that there was an inconsistency between the pedagogical knowledge and the technical knowledge required to benefit from technology in the language classrooms. Akayoğlu and Cirit (2017) investigated the preferences of pre-service language teachers regarding the tools integrated into their lesson plans and found that the participants mostly opted for tools that would support their teaching and learning practices through audio-visual materials.

The studies briefly reviewed indicate that pre-service and in-service language teachers adopt positive attitudes towards the use of technology in their language classrooms. However, there are also several factors that affect their attitudes and perceptions, such as the lack of training depending on their context, the technological resources available at schools, and the mismatch between what is included in the courses in teacher education programmes and the real-life situations at schools.

Many of these studies reviewed focussed on the beliefs and perceptions of pre-service language teachers mostly during their teaching practice or during the courses offered in their teacher training programmes. This study, on the other hand, attempts to investigate two in-service language teachers' views on the training provided based on their needs and requests, their willingness to create and use digital materials in their classrooms, and the factors that would affect their decisions. It is also important to note that this study concentrates on the participants' self-perceptions and self-reporting of their willingness and explanations of the factors involved. In line with this aim, the following research questions were proposed:

- What are the participants' views and suggestions on the training provided?

- Were the participants willing to create and use digital materials for their classrooms? Why? Why not?

- What are the factors that might affect the participants' use of the materials in the classroom?

2. Method

2.1. Setting

This research was designed as a qualitative case study exploring two in-service English teachers' views and experiences on the training designed based on their own requests and needs. The study was conducted following a one-hour seminar, which was held on the benefits of using technology in the classroom for fifteen teachers of English in Burdur, Turkey. The teachers were teaching English at middle and high schools, and several of them expressed their interest in learning more about the possible ways of infusing technology into the classroom. Based on the researcher's availability and the teachers' schedules, two teachers of English agreed to attend a series of workshops that would focus on creating digital materials using several web-based tools available on the Internet, such as English as a Second Language (ESL) videos.

2.2. Participants

Two male teachers of English, Yavuz and Ahmet (both pseudonyms) participated in the study. Yavuz was an experienced teacher with basic knowledge of technology such as word-processing and surfing the Internet. Yavuz had fifteen years of experience in teaching English at various state schools. Ahmet, on the other hand, was a novice teacher with three years of experience. However, his knowledge of technology was beyond Yavuz' skills, such as using several online applications to create digital materials for teaching and learning English. Both teachers were graduates of the Department of Foreign Language Education and were working at two different secondary schools. They were teaching different classes, which included sixth and seventh graders, whose levels of English ranged from beginner to pre-intermediate. In these classes, the aim was to improve learners' English by integrating four skills. However, the major focus was on grammar, vocabulary, and reading. Both teachers were also teaching the eighth graders, who were going to take a language test in which grammar and vocabulary knowledge played an important role in determining students' success through multiple-choice questions.

2.3. Data collection instruments

Data included the participants' journal for each session during the workshops and a semi-structured interview. For each session, the participants kept a journal in which they discussed the tool they learned about, the possible uses and challenges of using this tool, and how they could integrate it into their own classroom. The semi-structured interview was used to obtain information about these two teachers' views towards the workshops and the process in which they created digital materials.

2.4. Procedure

The training lasted for five weeks, each of which consisted of three-hour hands-on experiences on the use of creating CALL-based materials, with a total of 15 hours of lectures and tutorials. The following topics and tools were included in the training, as indicated in Table 1. It is worth mentioning that, even though there were numerous activities that could be created using numerous tools available, the topics were selected based on the mini-interview conducted with the participants to better meet their needs.

Table 1. The topics and tools introduced during the training based on the participants' needs

Week	Topic / Skill	Tools / Websites
I	Creating online classrooms and sharing materials	Edmodo https://www.edmodo.com/
II	Video quizzes/listening	ESL video https://www.eslvideo.com
III	Creating stories/writing	Cartoon Story https://www.education.vic.gov.au/languagesonline/ Make Beliefs Comix https://www.makebeliefscomix.com/Comix/
IV	Online quizzes/assessment	Kahoot! https://kahoot.com/

V	Creating worksheets/ grammar and vocabulary	The teacher's pet http://www.teachers-pet.org/index.php
		Reading worksheet generator https://www.education.com/worksheet-generator/reading/

After each session, the participants were asked to keep a journal and briefly discuss the basic features of the tool they had learned, the possible uses, and challenges, with a focus on how they could infuse it into their classrooms. If possible, they were also asked to integrate it in their class and to discuss their experience in the following session. The semi-structured interviews were held with both participants after the training. During the interviews, the participants were asked questions on their views on the training they had received and their own experience with integrating the tools in their classes, and they were asked to share their comments and suggestions. In lieu of taking notes during the interviews, which would make it difficult to focus on the details, the participants' responses were audio-recorded, and the recordings lasted for 25 minutes on average. The interviews were then transcribed in full and coded using Nvivo.

2.5. Data analysis

The data collected through the journals and interviews were subject to inductive content analysis. The journals and the transcripts of the interviews were re-read repeatedly in order to determine the common themes and sub-codes. These themes and sub-codes were hierarchically ranked. The emerging themes and sub-categories were checked against consistency by another expert in the field, with ample knowledge of inductive content analysis.

3. Results and discussion

The results of the study are summarised below. The brief statements of the participants are provided and categorised in relation to the research questions, and they are reported for each participant.

3.1. What are the participants' views and suggestions on the training provided?

Both Yavuz and Ahmet expressed the view that they considered the training rather short while acknowledging that they were aware of this before the training started. However, Yavuz said he believed that the content and the efficiency of the materials are more important than the duration of training. He stated the following:

> "Although the training was short, the content was very efficient as our needs and expectations were taken into consideration" (Yavuz).

Both participants expressed a more positive view regarding the efficiency of the activities and tasks in the training. For example, Ahmet, the novice but more knowledgeable on issues of technology, said:

> "The tasks and the activities were geared towards our needs. I, for example, needed interactive games for my end-of-the-lesson activities so that my students can recycle what they learned, and I learned a lot during the training" (Ahmet).

This finding is consistent with that of the studies conducted by Göktürk Sağlam and Sert (2012), and Akayoğlu (2017), indicating that language teachers have positive attitudes towards the use of technology, as well as the training regarding the integration of technology.

Additionally, both Yavuz and Ahmet expressed the importance of making the content of produced materials interesting and relevant to students. Yavuz, the experienced teacher, correlated the quality of the produced materials with the learners' success as he thought that this is the most important aspect of infusing technology into language teaching and learning. He stated that he focussed on the features of the tools provided in the training. He explained that he tried to make sure the content or the tool he prepared had the potential to help his students to retain the content longer than the printed materials, which helped them build confidence. In addition to what Yavuz proposed, Ahmet underscored the importance of the training from a teacher development perspective. Ahmet expressed the need for such training from time to time as technology is developing rapidly, and teachers also need to remain closely informed about the current developments in technology and appropriate pedagogy.

The participants' views clearly indicated the need to reconsider teacher education programmes and the courses offered to students regarding the integration of technology in language learning and teaching activities. As related research (e.g. Sharifi, AbuSaeedi, Jafarigohar, & Zandi, 2017) has revealed, computer-assisted instruction or using technology in the classroom has an overall medium effect on learners' development in English language; therefore, it is not possible to avoid the use of technology in the classroom. Being well aware of this, the participants stressed that teacher training courses should include the topics and tools that would be expected to be effective and applicable to the contexts or schools where prospective teachers are supposed to work in their future career. The participants also noted the importance of making the digital materials interesting and relevant to learning goals, which is among the basic language learning and teaching principles. These findings are consistent with those of the studies conducted by Egbert et al. (2002), Kılıçkaya and Seferoğlu (2013), and Uzun (2016). Moreover, the current study also stresses the importance of planning and conducting training considering the pre-service and in-service teachers' needs in different contexts.

3.2. Were the participants willing to create and use digital materials for their classrooms? Why? Why not?

Both participants were willing to create and use digital materials for their classrooms. However, they expressed different reasons for participating in the training. Yavuz, the experienced teacher, expressed that he needed the training more than Ahmet as during his undergraduate studies he was not adequately introduced to the use of technology for language learning and teaching, apart from the basic introductory courses to computers. More specifically, the courses covered the use of word processing skills and the use of presentation software such as Microsoft PowerPoint, which has also been confirmed by previous research (Uzun, 2016), and the use of the Internet. Therefore, during the training, he was more eager to learn how other tools could be used in his classrooms. Yavuz also noted that the use of computers for language learning and teaching was not common in the schools where he worked due to the lack of hardware and related software. Ahmet was also eager to create and use digital materials for his classrooms. Compared to Yavuz, he had more knowledge of tools available to create digital materials and knew how to deal with technical problems while using computers. Therefore, Ahmet benefited from training to refresh and update his knowledge of new and different tools in language learning and teaching.

3.3. What are the factors that might affect the participants' use of the materials in the classroom?

Both teachers raised concerns about the use of the produced materials with eighth graders in secondary schools. They both expressed the view that these students were going to take a language test in which grammar and vocabulary knowledge was vital and that they preferred to do activities such as answering multiple-choice questions on paper. Their students did not like the idea of reading and answering the questions which were prepared as online quizzes (Krajka, 2003) on the smart board, even if they were created to revise the previously learned items. Yavuz said that doing an activity on a computer appears like a game to language learners. He stated:

> "My students consider the activities that we did through the smart board entertaining and interesting. However, when it comes to a high-stakes exam, I mean, the language exam, I think the activities done on screen do not appear serious enough to them" (Yavuz).

Almost the same views were expressed by Ahmet, who said the following: "We are forced to follow an approach, teach-test-teach", which is one of the results of harmful washback due to the high-stakes exams (Kılıçkaya, 2016).

Unlike what happened in the eighth graders' classroom, both teachers expressed that when they used their digital materials with other students, especially with the ones at lower levels, they obtained more positive results not only in achieving the goals of the programmes but also in appealing to student desires. This might be because students do not worry about exams or grades at lower levels, they try to enjoy game-like activities without being aware of revising the topics or items they practised in previous classes. Both teachers also noted the importance of the decision regarding the use of technology in the classroom. Yavuz, for example, explained that he would not be using technology if he could achieve the same result or success by using the board or paper. Regarding this, during the interview, Ahmet explained:

> "It sometimes takes a lot of time to create an activity on a computer, and you realise that you can do the same thing by using several pieces of paper with no difference in terms of making the content interesting and obtaining the same results".

Both teachers believed that teachers should spend time on creating digital materials using the tools on the internet only if they believe and foresee that they will be able to produce digital materials that will lead learners to retain what they learn longer, in comparison with the paper-based materials or just the use of the board.

Ahmet also stressed the importance of reliability of the technological tools available in the classroom. Acknowledging that the Internet connection was not always reliable, he explained that he focussed on creating digital materials that did not require an Internet connection, as he did not want to spend time on the slow connection or lack of connection during the activity. Yavuz, similarly, said that he tended to create materials that would not require much in terms of the technology available. Although he explained that they had smart boards with speakers and projectors available in their classrooms, he tried to deal with materials that did not require an Internet connection.

The reasons or the factors provided by both participants are among those expressed in the findings of several studies (Aslan & Zhu, 2015; Garrett, 2009;

Merç, 2015). However, unlike the finding of the study by Merç (2015), which indicated the lack of the technological tools available in the schools, the participants in this study had sufficient technological tools. The concern was more related to the reliability of the devices and services available as they did not want to spend time dealing with technical issues.

4. Conclusions

The current study focussed on two English teachers' views and experiences in creating digital materials based on various tools and websites. The findings of the study indicated that the participants had positive attitudes towards infusing technology into their teaching practices and found the training efficient. The participants underscored the importance of making the digital materials interesting and efficient, which would help students both enjoy and learn the content and noted that teachers need to be updated through regular meetings and training in benefiting from technology in their classrooms. However, in a few contexts, although they were willing to benefit from technology, they could not realise their intentions for various reasons, generally related to the context of teaching. Since the findings of the study are only based on two teachers' experiences and responses, these findings might not be generalisable to all contexts. Moreover, it is also well acknowledged that the findings might not be generalisable to larger in-service English teacher populations. However, the findings can be transferable to other similar situations. In addition, the findings are believed to further contribute to the literature on participants' views on CALL training (e.g. Akayoğlu, 2017; Aslan & Zhu, 2015), specifically on creating digital materials and understanding the factors affecting their experience. Further research can be conducted with a large number of participants working with students at different levels and different needs and, can focus on the contents or syllabuses for training programmes considering the different learning and teaching environments where teachers are expected to work. Moreover, further research can also include the observation of the participants' classroom practices to determine to what extent they could put the theoretical knowledge into practice.

References

Akayoğlu, S. (2017). Perceptions of pre-service English teachers towards computer assisted language learning. *Elementary Education Online, 16*(3), 1220-1234. https://doi.org/10.17051/ilkonline.2017.330252

Akayoğlu, S., & Cirit, N. C. (2017). Preferences of preservice teachers of English in terms of CALL tools. *Mehmet Akif Ersoy University Journal of Faculty of Education, 44*, 146-161. https://doi.org/10.21764/maeuefd.331280

Aslan, A., & Zhu, C. (2015). Pre-Service teachers' perceptions of ICT integration in teacher education in Turkey. *The Turkish Online Journal of Educational Technology, 14*(3), 97-110. http://www.tojet.net/articles/v14i3/14310.pdf

Bates, A.W. (2015). *Teaching in a digital age: guidelines for designing teaching and learning.* Tony Bates Associates Ltd.

Egbert, J., Paulus, T. M., & Nakamichi, Y. (2002). The impact of CALL instruction on classroom computer use: a foundation for rethinking technology in teacher education. *Language Learning & Technology, 6*(3), 108-126. http://www.lltjournal.org/item/2409

Garrett, N. (2009). Computer-assisted language learning trends and issues revisited: integrating innovation. *The Modern Language Journal, 93*(1), 719-740. https://doi.org/10.1111/j.1540-4781.2009.00969.x

Göktürk Sağlam, A. L., & Sert, S. (2012). Perceptions of in-service teachers regarding technology integrated English language teaching. *Turkish Online Journal of Qualitative Inquiry, 3*(3), 1-14. http://www.tojqi.net/articles/TOJQI_3_3/TOJQI_3_3_Article_1.pdf

Kessler, G., & Plakans, L. (2008). Does teachers' confidence with CALL equal innovative and integrated use? *Computer Assisted Language Learning, 21*(3), 269-282. https://doi.org/10.1080/09588220802090303

Kılıçkaya, F. (2016). Washback effects of a high-stakes exam on lower secondary school English teachers' practices in the classroom. *Lublin Studies in Modern Languages and Literature, 40*(1), 116-134. https://doi.org/10.17951/lsmll.2016.40.1.116

Kılıçkaya, F., & Seferoğlu, G. (2013). The impact of CALL instruction on English language teachers' use of technology in language teaching. *Journal of Second and Multiple Language Acquisition, 1*(1), 20-38. https://files.eric.ed.gov/fulltext/ED570175.pdf

Krajka, J. (2003). On the web-making web-based quizzes in an instant. *Teaching English with Technology, 3*(1), 51-56. http://tewtjournal.org/issues/past-issue-2003/past-issue-2003-issue-1/

Merç, A. (2015). Using technology in the classroom: a study with Turkish pre-service EFL teachers. *The Turkish Online Journal of Educational Technology, 14*(2), 229-240. http://www.tojet.net/articles/v14i2/14225.pdf

Sharifi, M., AbuSaeedi, A. R., Jafarigohar, M., & Zandi, B. (2017). Retrospect and prospect of computer assisted English language learning: a meta-analysis of the empirical literature. *Computer Assisted Language Learning, 31*(4), 413-436. https://doi.org/10.1080/09588221.2017.1412325

Son, J. B. (2018). *Teacher development in technology-enhanced language teaching*. Palgrave Macmillan. https://doi.org/10.1007/978-3-319-75711-7

Uzun, L. (2016). The educational and technical courses in the ELT program in Turkey: do they contribute to ICT skills? *Cogent Education, 3*, 1141454, 1-12. https://doi.org/10.1080/2331186X.2016.1141454

Enhancing literacy and collaborative skills through blogging: the teenage language learner

Christina Nicole Giannikas[1]

Abstract

Blogs are considered to have made an intervention in many English as a foreign language contexts. The architecture of the platform is thought to give authorship, a readership, and ownership of one's work, and encourage collaborative learning. The present chapter focusses on an exploratory research study which took place in a private language school setting in Greece. The study included 52 teenage learners who were introduced to Edublogs for the first time. The aim of the study was to (1) determine the frequency and form of peer feedback, (2) investigate the impact of blogs on students' collaborative skills, and (3) to investigate the progress made in students' literacy skills with the integration of blogs in the curriculum. Questionnaires were distributed to examine participants' impression of blogs and the effect it had on their learning.

Keywords: teenage language learners, blogs, teaching literacy skills, teaching collaborative skills.

---

1. Cyprus University of Technology, Limassol, Cyprus; christina.giannikas@cut.ac.cy

How to cite this chapter: Giannikas, C. N. (2019). Enhancing literacy and collaborative skills through blogging: the teenage language learner. In C. N. Giannikas, E. Kakoulli Constantinou & S. Papadima-Sophocleous (Eds), *Professional development in CALL: a selection of papers* (pp. 145-158). Research-publishing.net. https://doi.org/10.14705/rpnet.2019.28.876

Chapter 10

1. Introduction

Traditional research and theory have generally centred their focus on how language learners can successfully develop the foreign language (L2) within the language classroom. However, research in the digital age has deemed this approach and understanding of language learning as restricted; this would imply that there is a limited range of discourse and literacy practices. Nowadays, technology, the internet, the media, and social networks provide greater opportunities and affordances for meaningful and authentic L2 use than what has been known to occur in the language classroom (Richards, 2014). A growing range of digital tools can be applied to offer learning opportunities that are likely to be interactive, social, and multimodal. One of the tools that can facilitate language learning and teaching is a blog; an easily created and updateable platform, which allows users to publish their writing online instantly (Bella, 2005). Blogging has emerged as a popular form of online discourse. More specifically, blogs are thought to improve students' literacy skills and take their creativity to another level (Melin & Laun, 2007; Ward, 2004) on platforms where "writing practices afford the learners an expanded audience and increased literacy activities" (Gebhard, Shin, & Seger, 2011, cited in Aydın, 2014, p. 248). Palombo's (2011) exploratory and design-based descriptive study reveals that young students' blog experiences facilitated their writing process and improved their written products. The blog content is the sole responsibility of the author, and their objectivity of what to write to engage their readership is in their control. The blogging experience in language learning provides the potential for alternative expression and reflection, leading to deeper learning (Bartlett-Bragg, 2003). Researchers have described successful attempts of integrating the blogosphere in the language learning classroom for the purpose of improving L2 writing and developing an L2 community of writers (Downes, 2014). Yang (2009) has found that interaction via blogs entails a social element where students engage in discussions of mutual interests and individual differences. Members of such communities "tend to get more involved than they do in other pedagogic and web-based environments" (Yang, 2009, p.13). In addition, as Goodwin-Jones (2003) has claimed, blogs encourage peer feedback and the articulation of ideas and opinions, they offer opportunities for collaborative projects and debates, and lead learners to engage in developing skills of convincing and argumentation. Evidently, the use of blogs encourages the revision of written materials, the giving and receiving of feedback, and increased participation in peer-review activities (Aydın, 2014, p. 250).

Even though blogs offer positive features of literacy and collaborative development in L2 learning, there is reluctance in using blogs with teenage learners for the purpose of improving writing skills (De Almeida Soares, 2008). The current chapter will present findings of the 'Blog On' project, a small-scale exploratory study conducted in a private language school setting in Greece. The study aims to contribute to the literature by presenting the impact blogs can have when integrated into the language learning curriculum.

2. Method

2.1. Data collection

The present exploratory study was triggered during an in-service teacher training programme the author had offered to private language school teachers in Southwestern Greece in 2015-2017. The in-service programme concentrated on educational technology and the integration of various digital tools in the language classroom. At the start of the programme, the language teachers were distributed an online survey which focussed on their students' pedagogical needs. All trainees expressed their frustration regarding their students' literacy skills and the fact that they had few resources to help their learners improve their writing. This frustration has been justified in the literature in a number of studies over the years. Writing is one of the most challenging skills to master in L2 learning. The skill itself is based on strategic use of the L2, which holds

> "structural accuracy and communicative potential (Dar & Khan, 2015; Hyland, 2003). [...] Writing is a cognitive process that *tests* memory,

thinking ability, and linguistic command to successfully express ideas (Kellogg, 2001; Geiser & Studley, 2002)" (cited in Fareed, Ashraf, & Bilal, 2016, p. 84, emphasis added).

In light of the teacher training survey outcomes, the present exploratory study was conducted in order to introduce language teachers to the blogosphere, in order to investigate its effect and study the development of the students' literacy and collaborative skills via blogs. For the needs of the research, the teachers were introduced to the benefits of using blogs with their learners and how to effectively introduce them to blogs and maintain their students' motivation to share blog entries throughout the academic year.

The present study focussed on 52 language learners aged 13-16, and the platform they used was Edublogs. The participating students were asked to write articles, essays (as requested for assessment purposes), and letters in their blogs as in-class activities. Then the students would provide feedback to their peers in the form of homework. None of the students had used blogs before, although they were all familiar with the concept. The research aims of the study were to:

- determine the frequency and form of peer feedback;

- investigate the impact of blogs on students' collaborative skills; and

- investigate the progress made in students' literacy skills with the integration of Blogs in the curriculum.

For the needs of the current exploratory study, data were gathered through a comparison of students' blog work and past in-class and homework assignments. For the needs of the on-site work, students were provided with a laptop. Additionally, the development of the students' collaborative skills was investigated by evaluating the form and frequency and quality of feedback students gave to their peers. Finally, questionnaires were distributed to examine participants' impression of blogs and the effect they had on their learning. The questionnaires were distributed at the end of the project. The data collection process lasted for 10 months.

2.2. Data analysis

ATLAS.ti 7 ©2013 (Scientific Software Development GmbH, Berlin) was used to analyse and code the students' writings (past and blog writings). The analytical process, based on principles of grounded theory (Charmaz, 2006; Glaser, 1992), was iterative and abductive (Dörnyei, 2007), and the data analysis involved a number of readings of the data entries and progressive refining of emerging categories. The procedure was carried out as follows (based on Giannikas, 2013):

- an initial reading of the students' written work was conducted. This process allowed the author to become familiar with the quality of the writings;

- the texts were re-read and thoughts were annotated in the margin. The text was examined closely to facilitate a micro-analysis of data;

- peer feedback frequency and repetition was measured and calculated; and

- results were analysed and organised according to the participating students' levels.

Past writing assignments were compared to blog entries in order to measure L2 literacy development. The analysis of past writing assignments followed the same procedure. The questionnaires were distributed on a hard copy, which the students preferred. The questionnaire data were transferred on a spreadsheet and calculated on Excel, where tables and charts were developed based on the data.

2.3. Setting the scene

Before the data collection commenced, teachers were introduced with the blogosphere; the teachers were asked to set the scene for their students in order to ease the students into their new writing tool. More specifically, they were asked to give the students a virtual tour of Edublogs and train them on how to use its features in-class.

Following the virtual presentation, the teachers were requested to assist students with the basic mechanics of the blogosphere, which would be to help set up an account and personalising it in terms of digital content. Students were also introduced to the concept of plagiarism. It was explained that students who plagiarised would immediately be asked to remove the post and repost a new one. Teachers were also asked to provide clear guidelines of (1) the tasks students would be asked to deliver via blogs (as mentioned above) and (2) how to give their peers constructive feedback.

The feedback guidelines were concerned with students' organising their feedback and language/phrases they would be expected to use. Table 1 and Table 2 show the guidelines provided to students in class.

Table 1. The dos and don'ts of planning our feedback

Dos	Don'ts
Explain what you noticed	Give your opinion
Show empathy and be kind	Hurt other writers' feelings
Help others reflect	Tell them what to do
Ask clear and inviting questions	Ask irrelevant questions
Praise the effort of others	Praise their ability

Table 2. A context for blog feedback

Sentence 1	Sentence 2	Sentence 3
I noticed that…	How might you…?	After reading your work, I realised that…
I observed that…	How could you…?	Now that I have seen your post, I think that…
I saw that…	What do you think…?	I used to think that, but now…
I realised that…	How did you decide to…?	Your writing has made me think…

At this early stage of the chapter it is important to mention that the participating students were initially reluctant to share their written work with their peers, in the fear of being negatively criticised. According to the questionnaire and feedback blog data, 60% of the students reported feeling exposed when they first published their work, whereas 40% of the participants did not attempt to share their first blog assignment. Out of the 60% of the students who posted their first assignment, only 10% gave their peers feedback and struck a discussion in the commentary (Giannikas, 2017).

The practitioners and the researcher experienced a standstill due to the students' attitude towards blogs, as the situation would not change for the first two weeks. This meant losing valuable time for L2 literacy development and data collection. In order to encourage the students to step out of their comfort zone and become more open to new learning possibilities, rewards were given to those who successfully completed a writing activity in a blog post. This worked positively resulting in 100% participation within four weeks of when the project commenced.

3. Results and discussion

3.1. L2 literacy development

Every week the students completed new blog posts that were later analysed. Within the first eight weeks, the students were recorded to improve their writing by 20% in comparison to their previous on-paper work. This was according to the teachers' feedback and assessment of their work. According to the students' feedback to each other on Edublogs, this occurred due to the fact that the online platform was more intriguing and prompted them to take notice of their own writing. Nonetheless, there were some setbacks in the students' writing in comparison to their past work. The data has been broken down in Table 3 and resembles the overall percentages of the 52 participating students over the 10-month period.

Table 3. L2 literacy development via blogs

L2 Literacy Skills	Increase	Decrease	No change
Advanced Vocabulary	20%	0%	0%
Recurring Errors	0%	45%	0%
Structure/Word order	20%	0%	0%
Grammar	15%	0%	0%
False translation	5%	0%	0%
Spelling Errors	0%	30%	0%
Coherence	40%	0%	0%

As displayed in Table 3, there have been important changes in the students' writing during the time of the study. According to the data, a 15-20% increase is seen in the use of advanced vocabulary, structure/word order, and grammar. Although the number may not be that high, this is an important development since there was no specific discussion or segment in the language lessons where the students would have been exposed to more grammar, vocabulary or structure than usual. This indicates that the students may have taken more time to compile their writing and also used the internet as a source of information and inspiration. Additionally, there was a significant increase in the coherence of the students' writing (40%). Students were calculated to plan and organise their work better and use linking words more frequently. Based on the comparison of the past and present writing assignments, students were more efficient presenting their work accurately in their blog entries. The current development connects to the fact that the students had an audience. It was detected in the peer feedback that coherence was an issue, especially during the first three months of the project. Gradually, students/writers made an effort to be understood by their audience. Spelling and recurring errors were recorded to have a 30% and 40% decrease respectively. This is a noteworthy development as it allows ample room for improvement. Students were prompted to pay attention to their errors, correct them, and memorise the correct version of a particular linguistic phenomenon in order to improve their overall writing. Nonetheless, the participants were not accustomed to using laptops to complete writing assignments in the L2. This resulted to students making a number of typos (rare spelling mistakes, no space between words, not using capital letters when starting a sentence). Peer and teacher feedback encouraged proofreading before publishing a blog post. By the end of the project, however, it was noted that these typos were sparsely seen. Nonetheless, this is a new issue that needs to be taken into consideration when investigating L2 writing assignments in the digital age.

3.2. Peer feedback via blogs

One of the most powerful elements of integrating blogs with the teenage learners was peer feedback. Due to the feedback and the fact that now the participants were writing for a wider audience, students were prompted to shift their mindset in order to write with a larger scope. This was beneficial for the student who received the feedback and for the students giving it. Even though the term *feedback* leads to the notion of assessment, for the needs of the present chapter, feedback will be referring to comments on learners' contributions that are not associated with formal grading, but to help writers improve their L2 literacy skills and for all students to engage in meaningful and pedagogical interaction.

Nonetheless, peer feedback was not a simple task for the students in the specific context. Students reported that, even though they were given guidelines, they did not know what to say in their comments and feared that negative feedback could bring out negativity outside and inside the language classroom. The feedback process took time, however, once students became engaged in the task, they developed a feeling of how to best approach their peers and what to say to help them, as seen in the following samples (copied from Edublogs):

> "I really liked what you had to say about the pollution in our city, it is such a big problem. I agree that the government should help the people fix this problem, but how? What do you think? How can we help too?" (Student 14).

> "Your article is very good and I liked it very much. I think your English is very good and that your grammar is good also, but I think you could talk a bit more about your personal experience to make the article more interesting to the reader. Personally, I would like to know what YOU think" (Student 33).

> "Your writing is very good and everything you say is very interesting. I think you have developed the topic very well. If I were to say something 'negative' is that you make grammar mistakes. If you manage to improve your grammar you will get an A in the exams!" (Student 6).

It was calculated that blog entries had two to seven comments, and in none of the comments or replies was there any conflict recorded. Despite the promised rewards and interaction among students, 17% of the participants never gave any feedback nor interacted during the course of the research. When the students were asked why they insisted in not participating in this part of the task, they responded that they had nothing to share and that feedback was best given by the teacher. The specific students never commented on their peers' feedback to their work, and were the writers who had the fewest comments/peer feedback out of all the participants.

3.3. Questionnaire outcomes

The distribution of questionnaires was to assist the researcher in collecting data regarding the students' experiences as blog users. Evidence was collected relating to students' perceived benefits for learning and their opinions regarding the various writing tasks used in the project.

In Part A of the questionnaire, participants were asked about their prior experience with the use of computer-based applications, in particular blogs, their learning preferences, and their perceptions of the project after having been given an initial description. Part B of the questionnaire focussed on their general perceptions of blogs.

According to the data gathered, all students portrayed themselves as computer literate and used technology daily for private and educational purposes, although none of the participants had attempted to start a blog (whether in their L1 or L2). Table 4 displays the outcomes of part A of the questionnaire distributed to students.

Table 4. The students' perspectives: Part A of the questionnaires

Statements	Strongly Agree	Agree	I don't know	Strongly Disagree	Disagree
I enjoyed working on Edublog	42%	33%	0%	8%	17%
I would continue to use blogs in the classroom	48%	20%	2%	13%	17%
I will continue to use blogs for personal use/sharing	27%	25%	18%	25%	5%
Blog writing helped me improve my written English skills	38%	52%	0%	2%	18%
Writing in blogs helped me improve my vocabulary	22%	45%	8%	5%	20%
Writing in blogs helped me improve my grammar	10%	32%	2%	18%	38%
I am a more confident writer now	44%	24%	0%	12%	20%
I prefer writing on blogs than on paper	30%	34%	2%	17%	17%
I benefited from the Blog project	45%	34%	0%	4%	17%

The vast majority of the participants believed that their language learning and writing skills developed through Blogging and their participation in the project. A high percentage of the students saw a difference in their writing as far as vocabulary (Strongly Agree: 22%; Agree: 45%) and grammar (Agree: 32%) were concerned. This implies that the students not only improved in these domains, but their involvement in their own work and the peer feedback they received helped them notice, not only their errors, but their progress as well. They became very aware of the language they were using and how they were using it. Another important development is that the students stated they preferred to write their assignments on blogs rather than using pen and paper (Strongly Agree: 30%; Agree: 34%). This could mean new writing opportunities for the students and new teaching approaches for the practitioners.

In Part B, students were given the opportunity to elaborate more on the use of blogging in their language learning, including the advantages and disadvantages of using Blogs. The disadvantages the students pinpointed were that they (30%)

were still reluctant to share their work with their peers and receive feedback from them. According to 22% of the respondents, they were not convinced that their feedback would be as useful as their teachers'. Furthermore, 25% of the students claimed that completing their written work on a piece of paper was more reliable than on Edublog, as they would not need to rely on their internet connection. Nonetheless, all students agreed that the advantages outweigh the disadvantages. More specifically, 57% of the students had a very positive stance towards the use of blogs and the advantages they offer in their language learning. Here are some of the students' comments:

> "I really think it did me a lot of good. I was very afraid to use it [Edublogs] at first, but now I don't mind if other people see my work. We are all students and we are learning so there is nothing to be afraid of" (Student 50).

> "Blogging is a great and modern way to learn English and improve your writing. I am glad we started using them and I hope we continue because I have learned a lot during this time" (Student 28).

> "Blogging is the new way to learn how to write. You can be creative and use different online resources that will give you ideas and help you develop a topic. You can add pictures, links, clips, which you cannot do on a piece of paper. I think my writing now has more colour" (Student 15).

> "One of its [Edublogs] greatest advantage is that I can share my ideas with my classmates and I can keep up with their work. I know what everyone is doing and what they find difficult and I don't feel it's just me" (Student 51).

4. Conclusions

The present study displays the effects of integrating blogs as a virtual learning environment with teenage language learners. The participating students did not have any previous blogging experience, which was why careful consideration was given to the methods of its integration. The results have shown that digital tools, such as blogs, can help today's language learners improve their literacy and collaborative skills in a motivating and efficient manner. Learners were recorded to step out of their comfort zone, take ownership of their work, and take risks writing in the L2, and share it with others.

Acknowledgements

I would like to wholeheartedly thank the teachers and the students who so willing took part in the study. Their contribution and input shed light on alternative aspects of literacy development in the L2. Additionally, they are an inspiration to others as they embraced an alternative learning/teaching approach to improve and progress.

References

Aydın, S. (2014). The use of blogs in learning English as a foreign language. *Mevlana International Journal of Education (MIJE)*, 4(1), 244-259. https://files.eric.ed.gov/fulltext/ED545624.pdf

Bartlett-Bragg, A. (2003). Blogging to learn. *Flexible Learning in VET*, 4, 1-10.

Bella, M. (2005). Weblogs in education. In B. Hoffman (Ed.), *Encyclopedia of educational technology*. http://www.etc.edu.cn/www/eet/eet/articles/blogsined/start.htm

Charmaz, K. (2006). *Constructing grounded theory: a practical guide through qualitative analysis*. Sage.

Dar, M. F., & Khan, I. (2015). Writing anxiety among public and private sectors Pakistani undergraduate university students. *Pakistan Journal of Gender Studies*, 10(1), 121-136.

De Almeida Soares, D. (2008). Understanding class blogs as a tool for language development. *Language Teaching Research*, 12(4), 517-533. https://doi.org/10.1177/1362168808097165

Dörnyei, Z. (2007). *Research methods in applied linguistics*. Oxford University Press.

Downes, P. (2014). *Access to education in Europe: a framework and agenda for system change*. Springer Verlag. https://doi.org/10.1007/978-94-017-8795-6

Fareed, M., Ashraf, A., & Bilal, M. (2016). ESL learners' writing skills: problems, factors and suggestions. *Journal of Education and Social Science, 4*(2), 82-93. https://doi.org/10.20547/jess0421604201

Gebhard, M., Shin, D. S., & Seger, W. (2011). Blogging and emergent L2 literacy development in an urban elementary school: a functional perspective. *CALICO Journal, 28*(2), 278-307.

Geiser, S., & Studley, R. (2002). UC and the SAT: predictive validity and differential impact of the SAT I and SAT II at the University of California. *Educational Assessment, 8*(1), 1-26. https://doi.org/10.1207/S15326977EA0801_01

Giannikas, C. N. (2013). *Early language learning within a Greek regional context.* PhD Thesis. London Metropolitan University, United Kingdom.

Giannikas, C. N. (2017). *Welcome to the blogosphere: improving teenage learners' literacy and collaborative skills.* CyTEA Proceedings.

Glaser, B. G. (1992). *Basics of grounded theory analysis: emergence vs. forcing.* Sociology Press.

Goodwin-Jones, R. (2003). Blogs and wikis: environments for online collaboration. *Language Learning and Technology, 7*(2), 12-16.

Hyland, K. (2003). *Second language writing.* Cambridge University Press. https://doi.org/10.1017/CBO9780511667251

Kellogg, R. T. (2001). Long-term working memory in text production. *Memory and Cognition, 29*(1), 43-52. https://doi.org/10.3758/BF03195739

Melin, C., & Laun, J. (2007). Going contemporary in the intermediate-advanced curriculum. *Die Unterrichtspraxis / Teaching German, 40*(1), 1-8. https://doi.org/10.1111/j.1756-1221.2007.tb00025.x

Palombo, M. S. (2011). *Teaching persuasive writing with a class blog: an exploratory study in an urban sixth grade classroom*, ProQuest LLC. Ed.D. Dissertation. Harvard University.

Richards, J. (2014). The changing face of language learning: learning beyond the classroom. *RELC Journal, 46(*1), 5-22. https://doi.org/10.1177/0033688214561621

Ward, J. M. (2004). Blog assisted language learning. Push button publishing for the pupil. *TEFLWeb Journal*, 3/1.

Yang, S. (2009). Using blogs to enhance critical reflection and community of practice. *Educational Technology & Society, 12*(2), 11-21.

11. How different are European and American foreign language teachers regarding the use of ICT in task-based language learning? Beliefs, attitudes and practices in the classroom

António Lopes[1]

Abstract

The results of a transatlantic survey on technology-mediated Task-Based Language Learning (TBLL) are presented and discussed. The study was conducted within the scope of the European-funded Pan-European Task Activities for Language Learning (PETALL) project. The aim was to determine the teachers' acquaintance with TBLL and with the potential of Information and Communications Technology (ICT) for enhancing that approach. The survey also allowed us to characterise the teaching practices used in the language classroom in terms of this approach. As it was also possible to compare the responses from several countries, including the US, this chapter looks into the differences in beliefs, attitudes, and practices that exist between EU and US practitioners. The analysis of the data (by frequency) shows that there is a difference between the US and the EU in relation to TBLL in terms of familiarity, conceptualisation, and forms of implementation in the classroom. There are also differences in defining the benefits of technology-mediated tasks, as the EU respondents put emphasis on the teacher's creativity and responsiveness to new challenges, whereas the US respondents underlie the importance of it providing

---

1. University of Algarve and CETAPS, Faro, Portugal; alopes@ualg.pt

How to cite this chapter: Lopes, A. (2019). How different are European and American foreign language teachers regarding the use of ICT in task-based language learning? Beliefs, attitudes and practices in the classroom. In C. N. Giannikas, E. Kakoulli Constantinou & S. Papadima-Sophocleous (Eds), *Professional development in CALL: a selection of papers* (pp. 159-179). Research-publishing.net. https://doi.org/10.14705/rpnet.2019.28.877

communication contexts closer to real life, as well as the opportunity for collaboration and mutual assistance.

Keywords: task-based language learning, ICT in language teaching, teaching practices, teacher training, teachers' beliefs.

1. Introduction

In early 2016, an international survey on technology-mediated TBLL was launched within the scope of the European-funded project PETALL. The importance of ICT in TBLL has been the subject of a number of studies published in recent years (González-Lloret & Ortega, 2014; Lai & Li, 2011; Martins, 2015; Roessingh, 2014; Schmid & Whyte, 2014; Schrooten, 2006; Thomas & Reinders, 2010). The purpose of the survey was, on the one hand, to determine how well acquainted teachers were with TBLL and with the potential that ICT has to enhance that approach, and, on the other, to characterise the teaching practices used in the language classroom in terms of TBLL and ICT. As this was an international survey, it was also possible to compare the responses from several countries, including the US. In the particular case of the present study, the aim was to learn about the differences in beliefs, attitudes, and practices that exist between EU and US practitioners regarding TBLL, and in particular regarding the use of ICT in TBLL, while probing, at the same time, their understanding of other approaches and methods.

There have been several studies conducted within the European context comparing foreign language teacher training in different countries (e.g. Eurydice, 2001), but studies between EU countries and the US do not abound. Allen (2013) carried out a study on the perceptions and beliefs about the development of language proficiency of a group of US teachers of French as a foreign language in the context of a three-week workshop in France. Although this was a transatlantic experience, the study did not seek to match the US teachers' teaching practices with those of their French colleagues, the aim being solely to find out whether such beliefs about the improvement of proficiency within the context of study abroad were compatible with the literature on foreign language teaching. Another study by Yturriago and Aguirre (2015) discusses the differences in the dominant frameworks of language acquisition, language teaching policies, and underlying ideological principles between North America (including Canada) and Europe. It further seeks to explain the differences in perspective in terms of teaching methodologies. Still, it offers a predominantly theoretical perspective, without actually delving into classroom practices. A relatively similar study by Cañado (2010) focusses predominantly on foreign language teaching in the context of higher education and seeks to understand the ways in which globalisation, technology, and competition end up shaping language teaching policy frameworks on both sides of the Atlantic. Based on the analysis of such frameworks, the author concludes that the best way to achieve significant reform in higher education language teaching is to transcend frontiers and to work towards closer collaboration, integration, and internationalisation. Although the paper mentions some methods and approaches that have gained a predominant position within those policy frameworks, no substantive information is given about the teachers' perceptions and what actually takes place in the classroom. This chapter aims to shed light precisely on those practices, more specifically in the use of ICT in TBLL, and on the teachers' own beliefs and attitudes towards technology-mediated tasks.

The main objectives of this study were to:

- determine how well acquainted US and EU teachers are with TBLL;

- pin down the differences in the ways TBLL is conceptualised in the US and the EU;

- identify what other methods or approaches are mostly used on both sides of the Atlantic; and

- ascertain in what way ICT is being used in TBLL in the US and the EU.

2. Methods

2.1. Type of quantitative research

This quantitative study gathered data seeking to support generalisations *to* and *across* groups of teachers from different countries (Pedhazur & Schmelkin, 1991, pp. 229-230). Nevertheless, as far as the external validity is concerned, one should always consider that "attrition is almost inevitable" (Cook & Campbell, 1979, p. 73). As the intention was to establish comparisons between variables, the study assumed a descriptive nature, and was mainly based on an analysis by frequency. IBM SPSS 23 was used for the statistical analysis of data. As far as validity is concerned, the ANOVA test was applied to determine if there was a significant relation between the dependent variable ('Country') and the independent variables – all questions on the teachers' knowledge of task-based language learning, and questions about (1) the teachers' awareness of the potential of ICT in the language classroom and (2) the strategies to circumvent the lack of ICT resources in the classroom. Table 1 shows a significance level of .003.

Table 1. Results of the ANOVA test

ANOVA							
Model		Sum Sq	Df	Mean Sq	Z	Sig.
1	Regression	4.327	15	.288	2.404	.003
	Residuals	32.162	268	.120		
	Total	36.489	283			

2.2. Structure of the questionnaire

The data was collected on Google Forms from February 2016 to March 2017. The online questionnaire was comprised of 31 questions, six of them dedicated to the characterisation of the respondents (Sections A and B), nine to TBLL (Section C), five to ICT (Section D), eight to teaching practice (Section E), and three to training needs (Section F). In this chapter, the focus is placed exclusively on the questions related to the use of ICT in TBLL and the beliefs related thereto.

3. Results and discussion

3.1. Geographical distribution of respondents

The distribution of respondents from the US and EU is shown in Table 2 below.

Table 2. Geographical distribution of respondents

A3. Place of Origin					
		Frequency	Percentage	Valid percentage	Accumulative percentage
Valid	US	43	15.1	15.1	15.1
	EU	241	84.9	84.9	100.0
	Total	284	100.0	100.0	

From the total of 284 respondents, 241 were teachers from nine member states of the EU (namely France, Germany, Greece, Hungary, Italy, the Netherlands, Portugal, and Spain), which corresponds to 84.9%, whereas the teachers from the US totalled as many 43 (15.1%). Although the latter number is almost six times smaller than that of EU respondents, it should be noticed that, in terms of individual countries, the US came fourth, just behind Italy, with 54 respondents (19.0%), Greece, with 50 respondents (17.6%), and Portugal, with 44 (15.5%).

3.2. Methods and approaches

In order to determine how important TBLL was in regards to other methodological proposals, teachers from both the US and EU were asked about the diversity of language teaching methods and approaches they were familiar with (Question E7: 'Acquaintance with different methods') and the ones they claimed to use in the language classroom (Question E8: 'Use of different methods'). These were presented with a range of methods and respective definitions adapted from Shoebottom (2007), and partly based on Richards and Rogers (1986). They were listed in alphabetical order: Audio-lingual; Communicative language teaching; Community Language Learning; Direct Method; Grammar-Translation; Immersion; Lexical Syllabus; Natural Approach; Silent Way; Structural

Approach; Suggestopedia; Task-Based Language Learning; and Total Physical Response.

Each teacher is familiar with an average of 6.7 methods. However, only 4.1 (about two thirds) of such methods are used. At the bottom of the list of known methods come the Silent Way method, Lexical Syllabus, and Suggestopedia (between 24.9% and 31.6%), which also matches the list of the least used (between 7.4% and 12.5%). Also amongst the least used is the Immersion method (8.8%), although it is recognised by as many as 40.4% of the respondents.

Figure 1. Bar chart displaying the comparison between methods recognised and used (Questions E7 and E8)

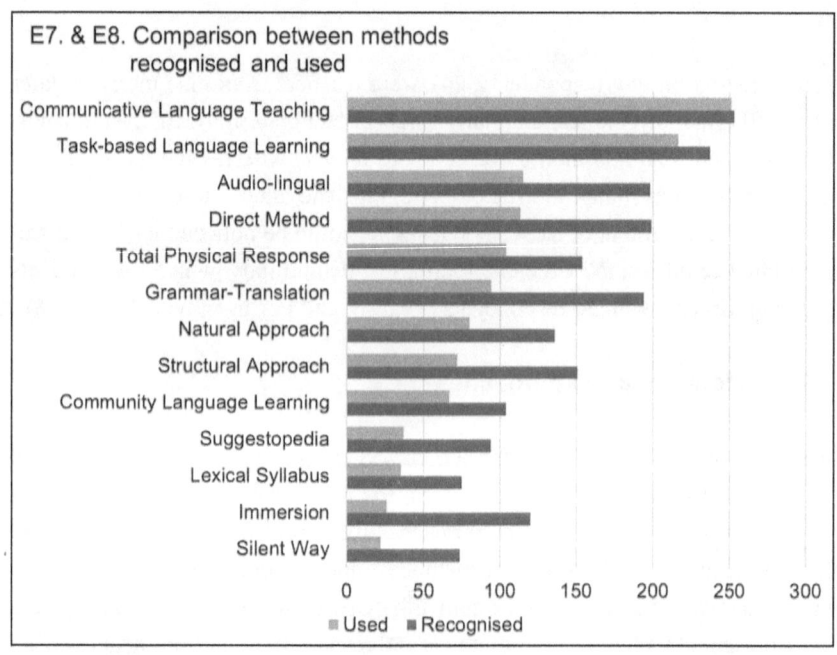

At the top of the list (Figure 1 above) comes Communicative Language Teaching, immediately followed by Task-Based Language Learning – recognised by 85.2% and 79.8% of the respondents, respectively, and used by 84.5% and 72.7%, respectively. Unsurprisingly, the difference between recognised and used in both of them is the smallest amongst all the other methods and/or approaches (0.7% in the first case and 7.1% in the second).

Grammar-Translation, the method associated with traditional practices, is one of the most widely recognised and yet only 31.6% of the respondents claim to use it. Similarly, the Structural Approach is recognised by practically half of the respondents, but those who use it are in fact below a quarter. Within the communicative paradigm, the Direct Method, the Natural Approach, and Immersion score significantly less than Communicative Language Teaching and TBLL, as far as use is concerned.

The differences between the US and EU figures cannot be overlooked. On average, US respondents claim that they are acquainted with one more method (6) than their European counterparts (4.99). This shows that American teachers are familiar with 46.1% of the methods listed, whereas European teachers claim to know only 38.4%. This somehow echoes the differences in the variety of methods used in the classroom, as the US respondents are more prone to diversify methods than the EU respondents (3.71 versus 3.11 – 28.5% and 23.9% of the total of the methods listed, see Table 3).

Table 3. Comparing the number of responses and percentages of US and EU respondents to Questions E7 and E8

Method	No. of US respondents who recognise the method	%	No. of EU respondents who recognise the method	%	No. of US respondents who use the method	%	No. of EU respondents who use the method	%
Audio-lingual	32	78.0	144	65.4	18	43.9	85	38.6
Communicative Language Teaching	37	90.2	186	84.5	34	82.9	189	85.9

Community Language Learning	11	26.8	75	34.0	10	24.3	50	22.7
Direct Method	32	78.0	146	66.3	23	56.1	78	35.4
Grammar-Translation	31	75.6	142	64.5	15	36.5	65	29.5
Immersion	29	70.7	80	36.3	5	12.2	21	9.5
Lexical Syllabus	4	9.7	62	28.1	2	4.8	29	13.1
Natural Approach	25	60.9	93	42.2	15	36.5	52	23.6
Silent Way	11	26.8	49	22.2	2	4.8	15	6.8
Structural Approach	27	65.8	108	49.0	13	31.7	50	22.7
Suggestopedia	11	26.8	68	30.9	2	4.8	29	13.1
TBLL	35	85.3	175	79.5	34	82.9	158	71.8
Total Physical Response	35	85.3	101	45.9	25	60.9	68	30.9
Total	320		1429		198		889	
Average (per respondent)	6.0	46.1	4.99	38.4	3.71	28.5	3.11	23.9

The most striking differences between the US and the EU in the methods recognised by the teachers can be found in Total Physical Response (where there is a difference of 39.4%) and Immersion (34.4%). US and EU teachers also diverge in their knowledge of the Natural Approach (18.7%), Lexical Syllabus (18.4%), and the Structural Approach (16.8%).

As far as the methods used are concerned, Total Physical Response is, once again, the method where the difference between the US and the EU respondents is more pronounced (30.0%), followed by the Direct Method (20.6%), the Natural Approach (12.9%), and Task-Based Language Learning (11.1%). The latter figure does not seem to be consistent with the result of the responses to Question C4 (Level of confidence in the implementation of TBLL), where US teachers' level of confidence scored lower than that of their EU colleagues.

3.3. Knowledge of TBLL

A more detailed analysis of their knowledge of TBLL (Question C1) shows that 67.68% of the respondents answered 'Yes' and that 27.95% answered 'Somewhat'. Only 4.38% answered negatively. This shows that what they claimed to be their overall acquaintance with TBLL (95.63%) is in sharp contrast with the percentages obtained in Question E7 (US=85.3%; EU=79.5%).

When comparing the results from the EU and the US, the percentage of EU teachers who claimed to be more acquainted with this approach was higher than that of the US. However, as the very concept of task lends itself to diverse appropriations, it was also important to see how the teachers' understandings differed from each other. In the next question regarding the meaning of the word task (C2), teachers were asked to choose one of the four definitions provided, which in turn had been borrowed from just as many authors offering distinct perspectives of the concept. The quotes were as follows:

> "A piece of classroom work which involves learners in comprehending, manipulating, producing or interacting in the target language while their attention is principally focused on meaning rather than form" (Nunan, 1989, p. 10).

> "A task is a work plan that requires learners to process language pragmatically in order to achieve an outcome that can be evaluated in terms of whether the correct or appropriate propositional content has been conveyed" (Ellis, 2003, p. 16).

> "An activity which requires learners to arrive at an outcome from given information through some process of thought, and which allows teachers to control and regulate that process" (Prabhu, 1987, p. 24).

> "A piece of work undertaken for oneself or for others, freely or for some reward" (Long, 1985, p. 89).

Nunan's (1989) definition came first (144 respondents=48.48%), and Ellis's (2003) came second (100=33.7%). Prabhu's (1987) attracted less than half of those who voted for Ellis's (2003) (44=14.81%). Only a residual number of respondents went for Long's (1985) shorter and somewhat vaguer definition (5=1.6%).

The comparison between the responses from the EU and the US (Figure 2) shows that the order remains the same (first Nunan's; second Ellis's; third Prabhu's). However, there were more US teachers subscribing to Nunan's (1989) definition (with a strong emphasis on a more proactive attitude on the part of the learner) than EU teachers (50.0% vs. 43.43%), whereas Prabhu's (1987) (which focusses on the teachers' control and regulation of the process) received more responses from the EU teachers (17.14%) than from the US (9.52%). Concerning Ellis's (2003) definition, no significant difference exists between both groups (US=33.3%; EU=35.7%). Only EU teachers selected Long's (1985) quote.

Figure 2. Comparing the percentages of US and EU respondents to Question C2

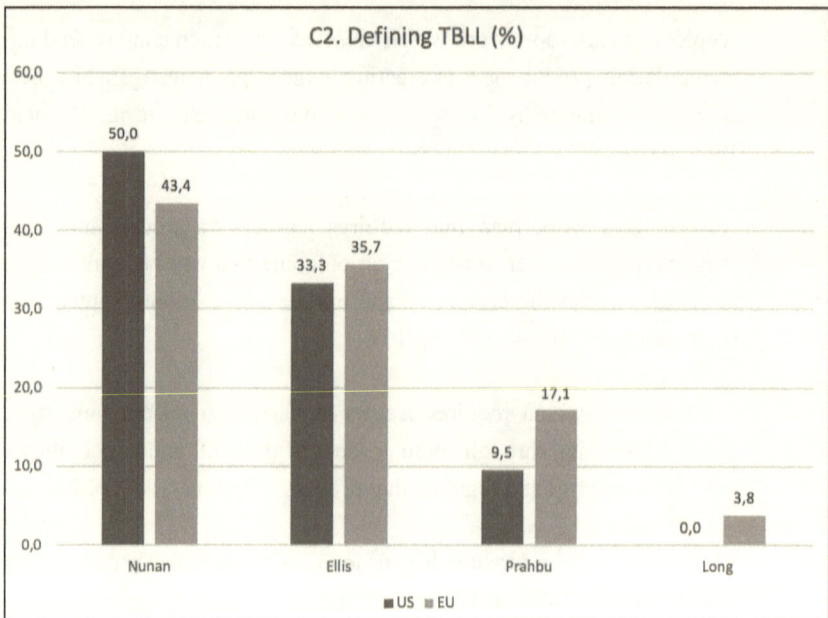

The antinomy classroom/real world was the focus of Question C3. This was a closed question with three options:

- (1) tasks require the learner to perform a behaviour similar to the one he or she will carry out in the real world;

- (2) tasks require the learner to do things that he or she will not do outside the classroom; and

- tasks require both (1) and (2).

Most teachers (71.38%) chose item (1), which signals a departure in perception from the traditional classroom activities and the role played by the learners in that context. A negligible number of teachers (1.01%) elected item (2), whereas over a quarter of the respondents (27.61%) chose (3), indicating that, though requiring a behaviour matching the circumstances of the real world, the task would still have to be implemented in the classroom. In this respect, there are no major differences between US and EU respondents.

3.4. Implementation of TBLL

Concerning their confidence in their own ability to implement TBLL (Question C4, in a five-point Likert scale), 5.7% (17 respondents) claimed they did not know how to do it. Most of them (53.2%) rated their confidence at 4 (124 respondents) ('I have a reasonably good idea of how to proceed') or 5 (33 respondents) ('I know exactly what it takes to implement TBLL'). Ninety-one respondents (30.63%) rated their confidence at 3, that is, they had 'grasped the basics of TBLL', but did not feel sure about how to put it into practice.

There are marked differences between US and EU respondents, as the level of confidence expressed by EU teachers and US teachers varies (Figure 3). Only 9,5% of the EU teachers chose 'Very well' (in sharp contrast with 16.67% of the US respondents). However, almost half (42.1%) chose 'Fairly well' (as opposed to 33.3%).

Question C5 asked teachers about the frequency of implementation of tasks in the classroom. Three quarters of the respondents (225) stated that tasks were implemented more than once per school term: 57 respondents (19.19%) claimed it was done once a week or more, 73 (24.58%) more than once a month, and the remaining 95 (31.98%) once a month or less. A minority of 16 respondents (5.72%) never implemented it at all, a number that is consistent with the number of those who answered 'not at all' in the Question C4 (Figure 4).

Figure 3. Comparing the percentages of US and EU respondents to Question C4

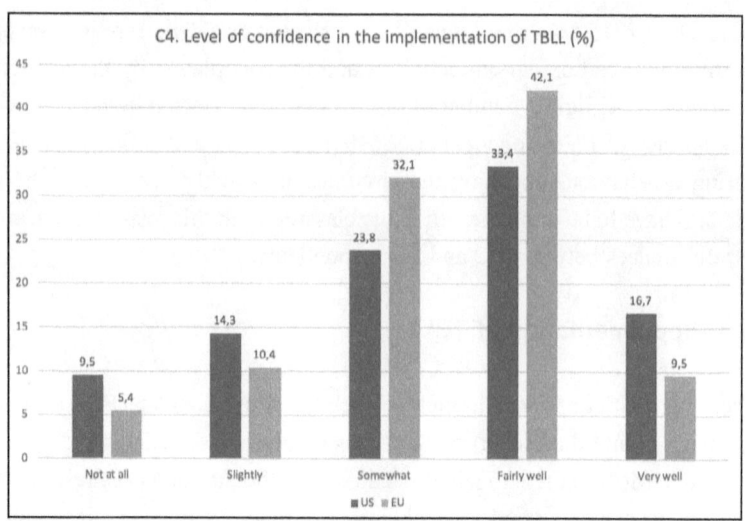

Figure 4. Comparing the percentages of US and EU respondents to Question C5

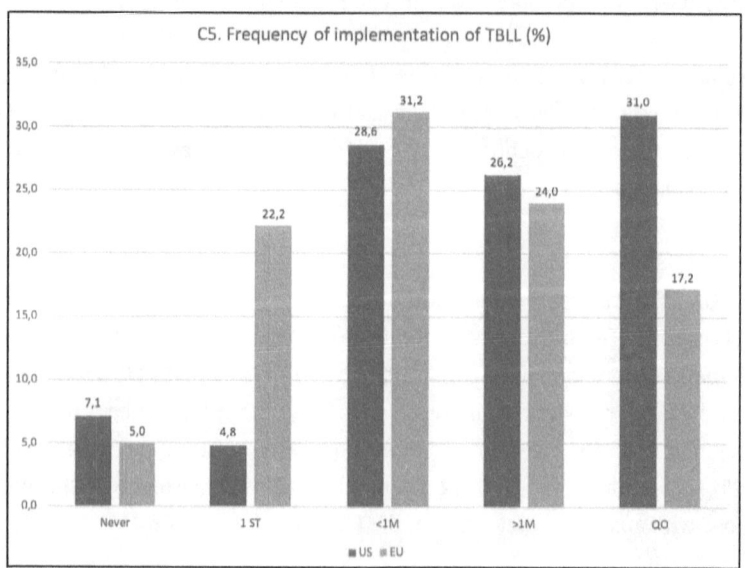

Despite the results obtained in Question C4, US teachers seemed to use task-based activities in the classroom more often than their European colleagues ('More than once a month' got 26.19% from the US against 23.98% from the EU; 'Quite often' got as much as 30.95%, as opposed to 17.19% of the EU respondents).

In Question C6, teachers were queried about the frequency of the use of ICT in the tasks. A significant part of the teachers answered affirmatively (Figure 5). 'Always' (23) and 'Often' (104) account for 42.7% of the universe, while 'Sometimes' accounts for 38.3%. Only 34 (11.45%) replied 'Rarely' and 22 (7.41%) 'Never'.

EU teachers seem more prone to include ICT in the tasks than US teachers, since the number of the former who answered 'Often' almost doubles the number of the latter (38.46% vs 21.42%). 23% more of EU teachers claim that they use it in relation to the US respondents (9.0% vs 7.3%).

Figure 5. Comparing the percentages of US and EU respondents to Question C6

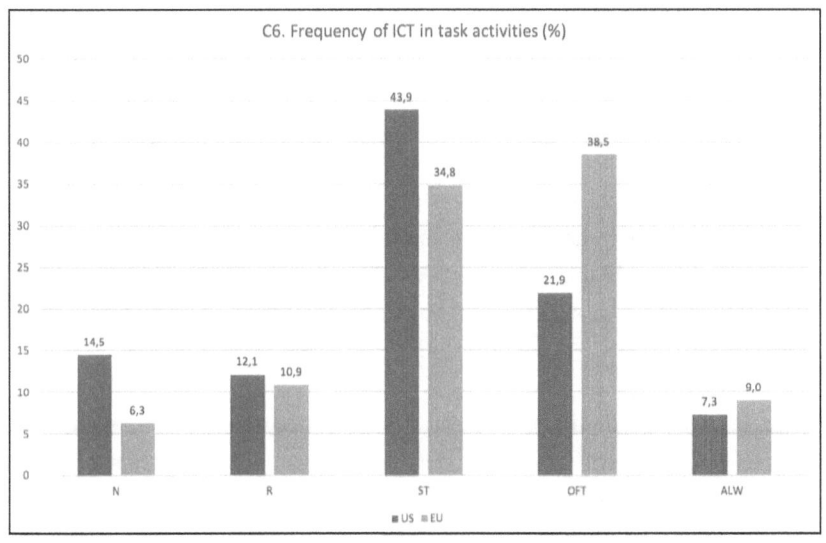

3.5. Perceptions of TBLL: benefits and challenges

In Question C7, teachers were asked to rank the positive aspects of technology-mediated tasks from one (the most important) to six (the least relevant). The aspects were as follows:

- (1) they lead to greater, more active involvement of the learners in the learning process;

- (2) they increase/promote the development of the learners' communicative skills;

- (3) they put learners in communication contexts closer to real life;

- (4) they give students autonomy and decision-making abilities;

- (5) they promote collaboration and mutual assistance; and

- (6) ICT+TBLL foster the teachers' creativity, adaptability, and responsiveness to new challenges.

Item (1) was ranked as the most important (28.3%), immediately followed by item (3) (24.6%). Items (2) and (4) came out with a tie at 16.2%, whereas only 5.1% chose (5) as the most important. These percentages show that teachers attach more importance to the learners' active involvement and real-life contexts than to issues of autonomy and collaboration. The promotion of the learners' communicative skills does not appear as a priority, nor does collaboration and mutual assistance, although literature often presents them as important features of TBLL.

As teachers ranked the items in order of importance, further calculations were made to determine which item scored the highest based on a sum of points (where the one ranked first was worth six points, down to the one ranked last, worth one point only). Item (1) came first with 1244 points, followed by (3), with 1184, (2) with 1102, (4) with 1089, (5) with 830 and (6) with 788. If we consider the first four items, the Standard Deviation (SD) is 63.1006141 with a Mean (M) of 1154.75, thus the SD being only 5.46% of M. Therefore, all four items are relatively close in terms of importance. Items (5) (promotion of the teachers' creativity, adaptability, and responsiveness), and (6) (collaboration and mutual assistance) scored markedly below the other items.

US and EU teachers responded differently to this question (Figure 6). More frequently subscribed by US respondents than their European colleagues were the notions that technology-mediated tasks deal with communication contexts closer to real life (respectively 76.01% vs. 61.17%) and that they promote the development of the learners' communicative skills (67.07% vs. 56.28%).

Figure 6. Comparing the percentages of US and EU respondents to Question C7

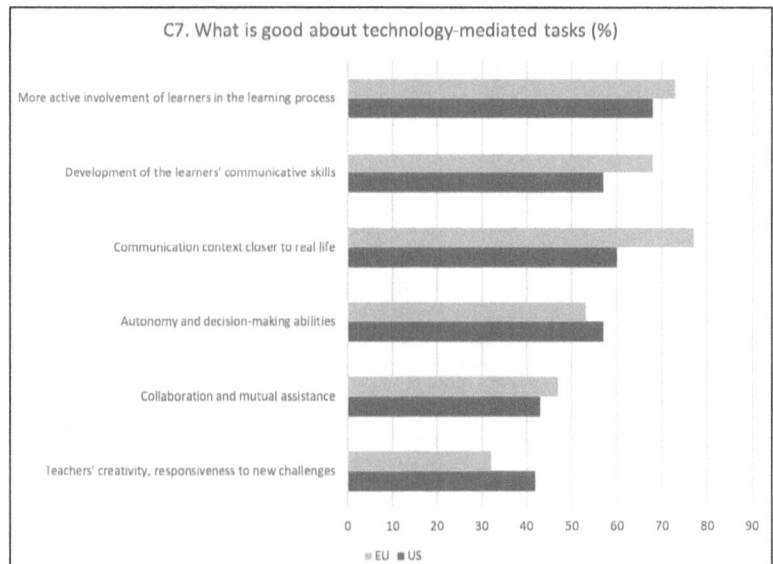

Question C8 was about the negative or challenging aspects of technology-mediated tasks. As in the previous question, options had to be ranked from one (the most important) to seven (the least relevant).

Chapter 11

The aspects they had to rank were as follows:

- (1) lack of knowledge of what TBLL entails or how to implement it;

- (2) difficulty in getting samples of good practice in ICT+TBLL that can meet my needs as a teacher;

- (3) difficulty in simultaneously monitoring the work of several groups of learners during the ICT+TBLL activity;

- (4) the learners' resistance to using the foreign language in the course of the activity;

- (5) the learners' lack of language/linguistic resources (vocabulary and grammar) to apply to the activity;

- (6) difficulty in designing and applying tools for evaluation that may enable the teacher to evaluate the learners' performance; and

- (7) difficulty in finding time to plan and prepare an ICT+TBLL activity.

Item (7) was by far the most important aspect (ranked 1st by as many as 22.9% of the respondents), more than 8% higher than Item (3) (ranked second by 14.5%). The variance of the remaining five items is of 0.5096, with a standard variation of only 0.713862, meaning that there is little significant difference between the percentages. Therefore, one may assume that the factors that stand in the way of teachers implementing technology-mediated tasks are not so much related to methodological issues (Items (1), (2), and (6)) or with the learners' limitations (Items (4) and (5)) as they are to pragmatic issues, in particular time management and classroom management (Items (7) and (3)).

As the items were ranked in order of importance, it was possible to ascertain, through the sum of points (where the one ranked first was worth seven points down to the one ranked last worth one point only), which scored higher. Item

(7) scored higher (1333 points), followed by (2) (1240), (3) (1216), (6) (1213), (5) (1191), (4) (1145), and finally (1) (978). With the exclusion of the latter, the SD is 57.22 with an M of 1223, SD being 4.68% of M. Therefore, the first six items are close in terms of importance. Items (1) and (6) are markedly below the other items.

A comparison between EU and US responses shows that differences are more marked in items (7) and (6), where US teachers seem more concerned about time management (84.96%) and the evaluation tools (72.36%), than the EU teachers (68.78% and 62.78%, respectively, see Figure 7).

Figure 7. Comparing the percentages of US and EU respondents to Question C8

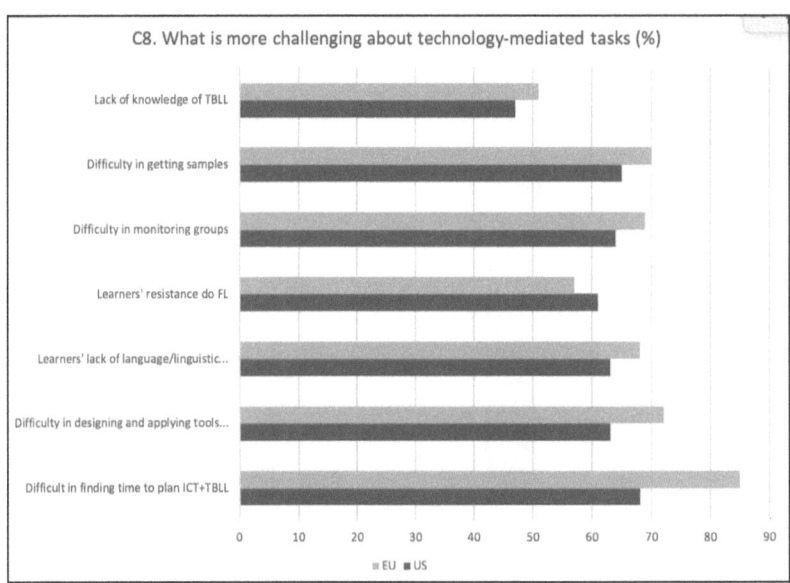

Question C9 addressed four general dimensions of ICT that teachers most value in TBLL activities. The dimensions were *Memory*, *Communication*, *Construction*, and *Process*. The most valued dimension was *Communication*, with 45% (in sharp contrast with the results of Question C7, where only 16.4% of the teachers claimed that ICT-based tasks promoted the development of the learners' communicative skills). *Process* achieved 29% and *Construction* 23%. *Memory* only scored 3%.

Again, as the items were ranked in order of importance, the sum of points was also calculated (where the one ranked first was worth four points down to the one ranked last worth one point only). Here the differences between *Communication* (930 points), *Process* (869), and *Construction* (788) are less marked. *Memory* (453) is still well off the mark. With the exclusion of the latter, the SD is 58.16 with an M of 862.33, thus the SD being 6.74% of M. Therefore, the weight of each of the first three items is relatively homogeneous.

There are no significant differences between US and EU respondents (Figure 8). However, as far as the *Communication* dimension is concerned, US teachers are more inclined to prefer it (58.94% vs. 47.38% of EU respondents).

Figure 8. Comparing the percentages of US and EU respondents to Question C9

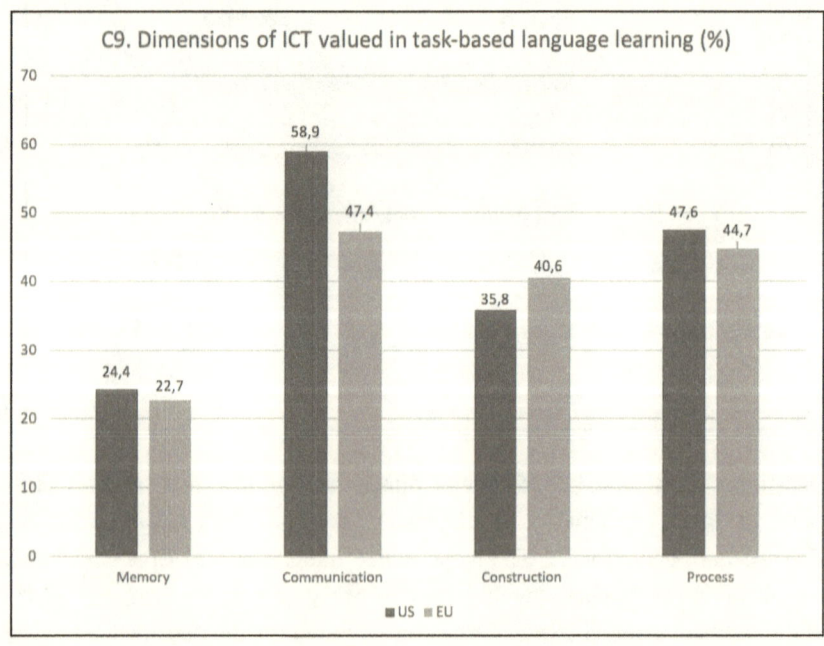

In order to establish the importance that teachers attach to ICT in the classroom, teachers were queried about the exploitation of the potential of technology in their teaching practice regardless of method or approach (Question D1); 90.24% stated that they exploit it. Nevertheless, EU teachers are slightly more prone to do it (92.3%) than their US peers (81.0%).

These figures match those of multiple choice Question D2 ('Do you believe that it is possible to circumvent the lack of ICT resources at school?'); 63.30% stated that, even if the school's resources were very limited, there would always be the chance to use ICT in the language classroom, though severely restricting their options. 28.62% chose 'Sure', while only 8.08% remained pessimistic, believing that there were no alternatives to school resources. Here US respondents were slightly more positive, as seen in Figure 9 below.

Figure 9. Comparing the percentages of US and EU respondents to Question D2

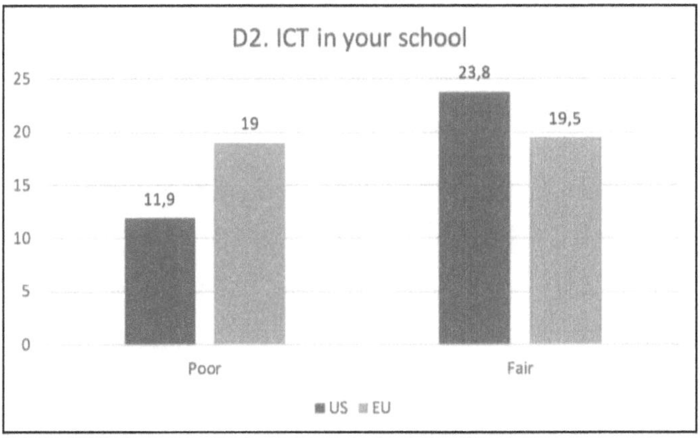

4. Conclusion

TBLL has now become one of the most used methods, regardless of it being in the US or the EU, although there is a higher percentage of US teachers using TBLL, and slightly higher percentage of EU teachers who prefer communicative language teaching. Nevertheless, only about half of both EU and US respondents (52%) claim they are confident about how to implement TBLL in the classroom. Data also show that ICT is used in TBLL on a regular basis, although US teachers are slightly less prone to exploit the potential of ICT in language learning. The vast majority of teachers (90%) also often make other uses of ICT in the language classroom, as they believe that ICT-based activities can be carried out without having to rely heavily on the school resources (92%). Still, US teachers claim to be less dependent on school by a margin of almost ten percentage points in relation to their EU counterparts. There are also significant differences when it comes to defining what is good about technology-mediated tasks. EU respondents put emphasis on the teacher's creativity and responsiveness to new challenges, as well as on the development of the learner's autonomy and decision-making abilities, whereas US respondents underlie the importance of it providing communication contexts closer to real life, collaboration and mutual assistance, the development of the learners' communicative skills, and a more active involvement in the learning process.

Acknowledgements

I would like to thank Christa Doil-Hartmann, Ioannis Karras, Amy Nocton, Raúl Ruiz-Cecilia, Carla Marello, and Marija Dragutinovic for their invaluable input.

References

Allen, L. Q. (2013). Teachers' beliefs about developing language proficiency within the context of study abroad. *System, 41*(1), 134-148. https://doi.org/10.1016/j.system.2013.01.020

Cañado, M. L. P. (2010). Globalisation in foreign language teaching: establishing transatlantic links in higher education. *Higher Education Quarterly, 64*(4), 392-412. https://doi.org/10.1111/j.1468-2273.2010.00451.x

Cook, T. D., & Campbell, D. T. (1979). *Quasi-experimentation: design & analysis issues from field settings.* Houghton Mifflin Company.

Ellis, R. (2003). *Task-based language learning and teaching.* Oxford University Press.

Eurydice. (2001). *Foreign language teaching in schools in Europe*. EURYDICE.

González-Lloret, M., & Ortega, L. (Eds). (2014). *Technology-mediated TBLT: researching technology and tasks*. John Benjamins. https://doi.org/10.1075/tblt.6

Lai, C., & Li, G. (2011). Technology and task-based language teaching: a critical review. *CALICO Journal, 28*(2), 498-521. https://doi.org/10.11139/cj.28.2.498-521

Long, M. (1985). *A role for instruction in second language acquisition*. Multilingual Matters.

Martins, M. (2015). How to effectively integrate technology in the foreign language classroom for learning and collaboration. *Procedia - Social and Behavioral Sciences (International Conference on New Horizons in Education, Paris, France), 174*, 77-84. https://doi.org/10.1016/j.sbspro.2015.01.629

Nunan, D. (1989). *Designing tasks for a communicative classroom*. Cambridge University Press.

Pedhazur, E., & Schmelkin, L. (1991). *Measurement, design, and analysis: an integrated approach*. Psychology Press.

Prabhu, N. S. (1987). *Second language pedagogy*. Oxford University Press.

Richards, J., & Rogers, T. (1986). *Approaches and methods in language teaching: a description and analysis*. Cambridge University Press.

Roessingh, H. (2014). Teachers' roles in designing meaningful tasks for mediating language learning through the use of ICT: a reflection on authentic learning for young ELLs. *Canadian Journal of Learning and Technology, 40*(1), 1-24.

Schmid, E., & Whyte, S. (2014). *Teaching languages with technology: communicative approaches to interactive whiteboard use*. Bloomsbury.

Schrooten, W. (2006). Task-based language teaching and ICT: developing and assessing interactive multimedia for task-based language teaching. In K. Branden (Ed.), *Task-based language education: from theory to practice* (pp. 129-150). Cambridge University Press. https://doi.org/10.1017/CBO9780511667282.007

Shoebottom, P. (2007). *A guide to learning English*. Frankfurt International School. http://esl.fis.edu/teachers/support/method.htm

Thomas, M., & Reinders, H. (Eds). (2010). *Task-based language learning and teaching with technology*. Continuum.

Yturriago, J., & Aguirre, S. (2015). Language teaching methodologies and ideologies in the United States and the Eurozone: a comparison study. *ICERI15 Proceedings* (pp. 7089-7097).

2. #SLA: the impact of study abroad on negotiation of identity on social networking sites

Chika Kitano[1], Daniel J. Mills[2], and Megumi Kohyama[3]

Abstract

This chapter describes an inquiry into how Japanese university students who have participated in study-abroad negotiate their identity on Social Networking Sites (SNSs) when interacting informally in English with non-Japanese interlocutors. SNSs provide a unique opportunity for English language learners to practise their skills in an informal environment, and to maintain and develop social connections with non-Japanese partners. However, maintaining one's unique identity in these intercultural exchanges can prove difficult. The results of this research showed that a study abroad experience had an influence on students' usage of SNSs in English. This was evident in participants' selecting SNSs that were more commonly used in the country where they studied and adopting non-Japanese behaviours on these platforms. Participants expressed that a fear of flaunting their English ability acted as a barrier to usage, but the effects of this factor was reduced after their time abroad. Finally, participants found that cultural differences in the usage of SNSs caused some tensions, and forced them to evaluate their own cultural preferences and decide what behaviours to adopt from the target culture. While several studies have investigated SNSs for language learning (Ottoson, 2014; Waragai et al., 2014), few have explored identity negotiation in this context

1. Osaka University, Osaka, Japan; u280193i@ecs.osaka-u.ac.jp

2. Ritsumeikan University, Minami-Kusatsu, Japan; danieljmillsedd@gmail.com

3. University of Shiga Prefecture, Hikone, Japan; megumimillskohyama@gmail.com

How to cite this chapter: Kitano, C., Mills, D. J., & Kohyama, M. (2019). #SLA: the impact of study abroad on negotiation of identity on social networking sites . In C. N. Giannikas, E. Kakoulli Constantinou & S. Papadima-Sophocleous (Eds), *Professional development in CALL: a selection of papers* (pp. 181-196). Research-publishing.net. https://doi.org/10.14705/rpnet.2019.28.878

(Harrison & Thomas, 2009). Therefore, the following inquiry fills a critical gap in the research literature regarding this topic.

Keywords: identity negotiation, study abroad, social networking sites, Japan.

1. Introduction

For language learners, study abroad offers a unique opportunity to not only develop competency in the target language, but to also be immersed in a foreign culture and to cultivate personal relationships with individuals from the host country. In the past, once a student returned to their own country, it took a concerted effort to maintain these relationships. However, with the advent of SNSs, such as Facebook and Instagram, it has become easier for returnees to continue to develop social connections created after cultural contact and continue to benefit from the informal language practice these relationships provide. Research into the impact of social media use on language learning prior to, during, and after study abroad has been explored in several studies (Ottoson, 2014; Waragai et al., 2014). Yet, few inquiries have focussed on how Japanese learners of English negotiate their identity on SNSs (Harrison & Thomas, 2009). Due to the significance of identity negotiation in the process of language learning (Pavlenko & Blackledge, 2004; Pavlenko & Norton, 2007) and the potential of social media as an informal English-language learning platform, there is a need for further research on this topic.

The purpose of this research was to investigate how a study abroad experience affected students' usage of SNSs when communicating with non-Japanese interlocutors. In addition, the researchers investigated the perceptions of the participants towards SNSs for informal English-language learning, and the process by which they negotiated their identity on these platforms. The research questions were as follows:

- What were Japanese students' actual use of SNSs in English before, during, and after a study abroad experience?

- What were Japanese students' perceptions of the advantages, disadvantages, and barriers of SNSs for English language study following a study abroad experience?

- How did Japanese students negotiate their identities on SNSs when communicating with non-Japanese interlocutors before, during, and after a study abroad experience?

2. Method

2.1. Setting and participants

The researchers collected data from university students in a Japanese public university. There were seven participants (five male and two female); they ranged from 19 to 26 in age. They voluntarily accepted the offer to participate in the study when they took part in a guidance session for a four-week study abroad programme conducted in Australia. The aims of the study abroad programme were for the participants to improve their English skills and to gain credits during the period spent abroad. This study abroad programme, which took place from the 17th of February to the 17th of March of 2018, was established and supported by a national university, which the participants belong to. Among the participants, five were undergraduates, and two were graduate students. A wide variety of majors were represented among the participants, including foreign languages, law, biology, economics, and dentistry. In order to protect students' identities, a pseudonym was assigned to each participant. Table 1 provides demographic information collected from the participants.

Table 1. Participants' profiles

Pseudonyms	Gender	Age	Major
Noriko	female	19	foreign language
Suzu	female	20	foreign language
Masaki	male	19	law
Go	male	20	law

Yuta	male	23	biology
Kei	male	19	economics
Hiro	male	26	dentistry

2.2. Data collection

The researchers used a mixed-methods approach in order to triangulate the data collected. The quantitative data was gathered through a paper-based survey, and the qualitative data was collected through semi-structured interviews and email exchanges. The quantitative survey was administered to the participants after they returned from their study abroad experience. Qualitative data was gathered first in a pre-sojourn interview and then through a more extensive interview process post-sojourn. In addition, the researchers exchanged emails with the participants during the time they were studying abroad.

The researchers created a survey instrument based on previous models found in the literature (Toland, Mills, & Kohyama, 2016; Vasilopoulos, 2015). The quantitative instrument was developed in order to investigate the usage and perceptions of SNSs for informal English learning as well as various factors that contributed to identity negotiation on this platform. The survey consisted of five sections: (1) self-confidence and flaunting, (2) cultural contradictions and tensions, (3) perceived barriers to usage, (4) perceived advantages, and (5) actual usage. Scales associated with perceptions ranged from 1 (*strongly disagree*) to 5 (*strongly agree*). The usage scale also had five levels ranging from 1 (*never*) to 5 (*always*).

2.3. Analysis

The quantitative data was analysed through descriptive statistics, which involved frequencies and percentages. The qualitative data was analysed by thematic analysis. This process required the researchers to manually sort the data into categories they developed based on their reading of the pertinent literature. These categories corresponded to the sections of the quantitative survey: (1) self-confidence and flaunting, (2) cultural contradictions and tensions, (3) perceived barriers to usage, (4) perceived advantages, and (5) actual use. Among all seven participants' narratives, a limited number of excerpts was selected to clearly illustrate the process of the participants' perceptions and negotiation of identity according to each dimension. Interview data is presented in the brackets at the end of quotation. For example, (i8october18yuta) indicates that the narrative is quoted from the interview with Yuta on 8th October 2018.

3. Results and discussion

3.1. Research Question 1: actual usage

After returning from their study abroad experience, the participants were asked to gauge their frequency of usage of various SNSs pre- and post-sojourn. The following chart (Figure 1) indicates the mean score of the participants associated with each SNS. The first bar shows their perceived usage before studying abroad and the second bar demonstrates their usage after studying abroad.

Figure 1. Pre- and post-sojourn usage of SNSs

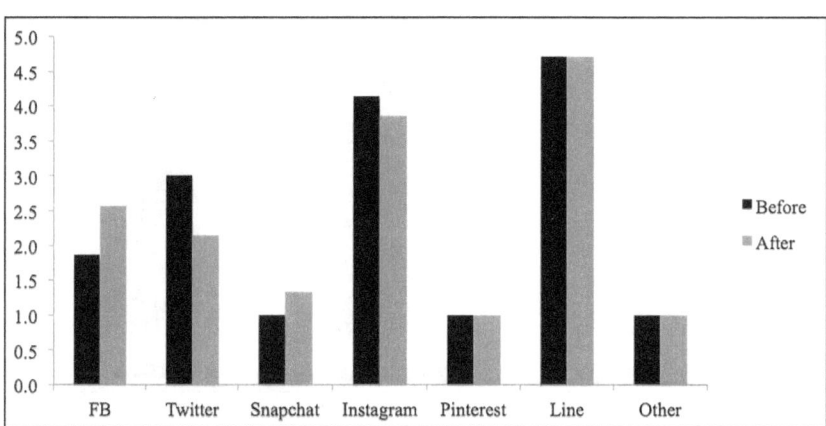

Note: Scale ranging from 1 *never* to 5 *always*.

The results seem to indicate that the experience of studying abroad influenced Japanese students' usage of SNSs. Snapchat and Facebook, two sites which are not as popular in Japan as they are in Australia (Sensis, 2017; Statista, 2018a, 2018b), showed an increase in usage. However, the usage of Twitter, which is a very popular SNS in Japan (Statista, 2018c), decreased among the participants. This may indicate that participants in the study were communicating more frequently with non-Japanese interlocutors and changed their SNS usage based on the preferences of their new communication partners.

3.2. Research Question 2: perceptions

Participants were queried regarding their perceptions of the advantages of using SNSs for informal English-language learning as well as the possible disadvantages and barriers to usage that were present when using SNSs for this purpose. Figure 2 displays the mean values associated with perceptions.

Figure 2. Mean value of perception constructs

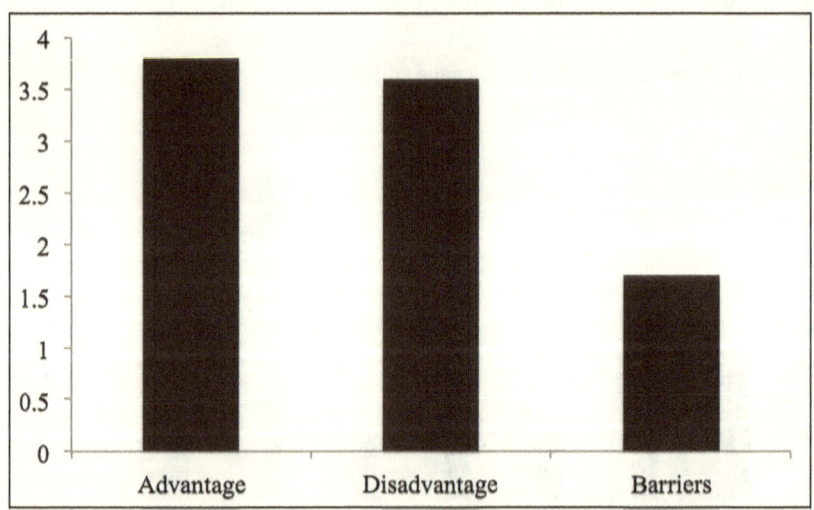

Note: Scale ranging from 1 (*strongly disagree*) to 5 (*strongly agree*).

3.2.1. Advantages

Six out of seven participants perceived that SNSs provided a good opportunity to learn authentic conversational English. For instance, Go stated:

> "I can really communicate, rather than just using expressions which I've learned through English textbooks" (i12april18go).

Noriko also demonstrated a positive impression toward SNSs, saying:

> "The English expression in usual mail messages is different from that we learn in school, isn't it? So, I want to know this type of English expression a little" (i25january18noriko).

The participants' narratives seem to confirm the work of researchers who regard SNSs as potential platforms for language learners to acquire informal language or real-life experience in a target language (Ottoson, 2014; Waragai et al., 2014). Furthermore, five out of seven participants stated that acquiring knowledge of internet slang was connected to learning authentic conversational English and that usage of SNSs would provide an opportunity to learn and practise these linguistic forms.

3.2.2. Disadvantages

Five of the seven participants agreed or strongly agreed that SNSs could serve as a distraction that would interrupt their study time. There seems to be strong evidence for this worry because several studies have shown that an increase in SNS usage is correlated with a decrease in academic performance (see Lui, Kirschner, & Karpinski, 2017). One possible issue for students that are studying abroad is that the usage of SNSs in their native language can rob them of the opportunity to be immersed in the target culture and language. While this sentiment was not expressed by any of the participants in this study, it is a factor that must be considered for future research.

While learning informal English and netslang was seen by several students as an advantage to the use of SNSs for language learning, four of the seven participants expressed the opinion that they may learn 'improper English' through the platform. Kei, a 19-year-old economics undergraduate, expressed his belief that much of the English used by native speakers on SNSs was "mechakucha" (i18april18kei), a Japanese word meaning chaotic or improper.

3.2.3. Barriers

Survey responses showed that participants believed their low levels of English and worries about privacy to be significant barriers to their usage of SNSs in English. The survey item 'When I read certain posts I get irritated' also received a high mean score among participants. Prior to the study, the researchers hypothesised that privacy would be a major issue for Japanese users of SNSs due to a cultural propensity to avoid sharing personal information with members outside of one's inner circle and the importance of saving face. A research conducted by Ishii (2017) showed that Japanese users of SNSs tend to avoid revealing personal information to friends online unless they also maintain a relationship in the real world.

3.3. Research Question 3: negotiation of identity

Identity negotiation is the process by which we establish our positions in relationships and the way we represent aspects of our identity, such as gender, ethnicity, and social position (Norton, 2000; Pavlenko & Blackledge, 2004). Individuals are constantly reshaping and repositioning their identities through the usage of language. Pavlenko and Blackledge (2004) insisted that "[n]arratives play a particularly important role in our account of negotiation of identities" (p. 18). They insisted that people negotiate their identities through "an interplay between reflective positioning, i.e. self-representation, and interactive positioning" (Pavlenko & Blackledge, 2004, p. 20). For Japanese students who have participated in a study abroad experience, SNSs can serve as a platform for this reflection when communicating with non-Japanese partners. The question of how English Language Learners (ELLs) negotiate their identities in informal settings is especially pertinent in the Japanese context where English is highly valued, yet, rarely used outside of classroom settings. Figure 3 displays the mean values of each construct associated with negotiation of identity.

Figure 3. Mean values of negotiation of identity constructs

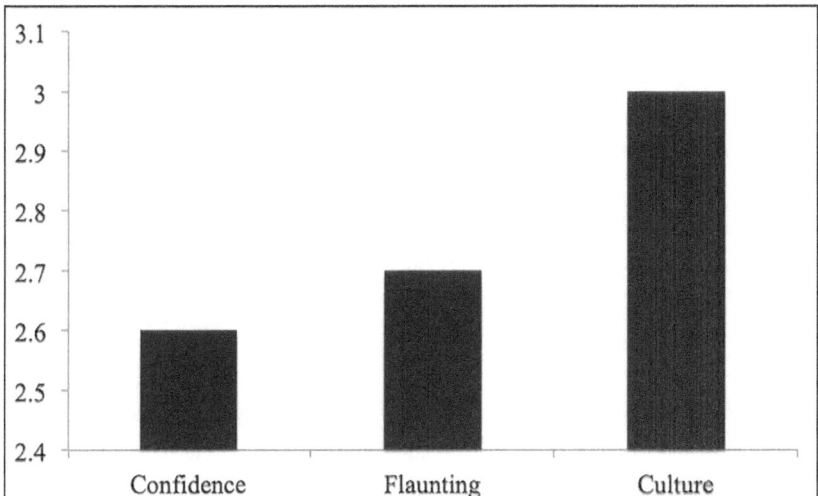

Note: Scale ranging from 1 (*strongly disagree*) to 5 (*strongly agree*).

3.3.1. Self-confidence and flaunting

In this study, self-confidence refers to a confidence in one's English skills or abilities in general. As SNSs provide a platform of self-representation, SNS usage in English is connected with how ELLs represent themselves as users of the language in public rather than mere students of English in private. Leis's (2014) research also indicated that students who display high levels of self-confidence in their English skills tend to use SNSs as a tool for English learning. Thus, self-confidence was chosen as a significant dimension of SNS usage in English in this study. Moreover, flaunting is connected with self-confidence. Yet, Vasilopoulos (2015) showed that fear of flaunting prevented his bilingual Korean interviewees from the usage of SNSs in English, even if they were fully confident in their English skills. Therefore, self-confidence and fear of flaunting seem to have an inverse relationship with SNS usage in English among learners of the language from cultures where flaunting is seen as a negative trait.

One participant who exemplified the dimensions of self-confidence and flaunting was Suzu. Suzu, a 20-year-old majoring in foreign language, was highly sensitive to flaunting in her pre-sojourn period. Because she attended an English conversation school for several years when she was a child, she had the feeling of being superior to other English learners. When asked about English classes in her junior high school, she said: "I was good at English" (i31january18suzu).

While she was confident with her English abilities, she was afraid of being seen as showing off her ability on SNSs. Furthermore, she strongly criticised Japanese people who, despite possessing low-level English skills, post something in English on SNSs.

> "It is not for improving (their English skills), but rather, like, they want to show off that they can post something in English" (i31january18suzu).

> "When they (Japanese people) post something in English, they must feel it is cool (to post in English). This is almost, I am just mocking them" (i31january18suzu).

She also negatively commented on the effect of the usage of SNSs on the improvement of English skills saying:

> "It can be to practise, but people post in English even if there are mistakes" (i31january18suzu).

As she had no relationship with anyone who used English via SNSs, she continued by saying:

> "If they have only Japanese followers, I am wondering why they post in English" (i31january18suzu).

Finally, she asserted:

> "I think almost everyone posted their experiences in their target language while they study abroad, but I have decided I will not do it if I study abroad" (i31january18suzu).

However, her perceptions and attitudes toward SNSs slightly changed after her sojourn. While studying abroad, for the first time, she made some English-speaking friends. It was the first time for her to make friends with whom she communicated only in English. Although, in her pre-sojourn period, she asserted that she would not post something in English, after returning to Japan, she changed the declaration.

> "Like, international friends started to follow my Instagram, so I'm thinking of using both, a little bit. I think it may be good to post something in both Japanese and English" (i4april18suzu).

In addition, she demonstrated that her perception towards SNSs also changed slightly when she was asked about the effect of SNS usage in English on improvement of learners' English skills.

> "Well, it's good if we post something after checking properly by ourselves" (i4april18suzu8).

In her pre-sojourn period, she thought someone must check her English grammar for her ability to improve when using SNSs. However, she came to realise that posting in English can be effective for English learning if the grammar is checked by the poster even if they do not possess a high-level of English skill.

3.3.2. Cultural tensions and contradictions

Cultural contradictions and tensions refer to issues arising due to cultural differences between Japanese society and the English-speaking society on SNSs.

Chapter 12

Hiro was a frequent passive user of SNSs prior to study abroad. He believed that SNSs could be a beneficial platform to learn English, stating: "I think I can learn, like, English slang" (i29january18hiro). However, after returning from study abroad he noted an important cultural difference in usage. He said:

> "My friends (in Australia) often post their faces on their SNSs" (i5april18hiro).

He posited that this behaviour represented a form of narcissism among non-Japanese people and a lack of shame. He further commented:

> "Men (Australian men) who are not good-looking guys post close ups of their faces. Even if they have a bushy beard at the time, they post their faces without hesitation" (i5april18hiro).

Observation of Hiro's Instagram account (with the participant's permission) showed that the vast majority of photos he posted were of food and nature, rather than people, compared to the other interviewees. This might indicate the Japanese people who are conscious about Japanese cultural norms tend to hesitate in sharing private information with outsiders.

Hiro's opinion was corroborated by another participant, Noriko. She commented:

> "I think many people (in Australia) are using SNSs to express themselves. For instance, my Australian friend posts her work on her SNSs" (i12april18noriko).

> "But, Japanese people post something, like, when they go to a cafe" (i12april18noriko).

It seems by "express themselves", Noriko means sharing private information. Although she recognised the varying usages of SNSs in English-speaking cultures, she has continued to mostly adhere to Japanese social norms on SNSs, even after her sojourn. This is evident from the content she posts, which tends to focus on subjects like what she ate or a place she visited and does not usually include pictures of people or sharing aspects of her life that she considers private.

The aforementioned observation and the narratives indicate that participants have not changed their attitudes toward SNSs although they were conscious about the cultural differences after their sojourn. This can be because the majority of their followers are still Japanese and they do not feel the necessity to change their ways of using SNSs. In this sense, the result shows that their identities as Japanese on SNSs have remained the same even after their sojourn.

Usage of internet slang was also perceived as a cultural contradiction and tension by some participants despite also citing it as a form of the language they wanted to learn by using SNSs in English. For example, Masaki strongly agreed with the survey question: I have experienced difficulties when using SNSs in English due to cultural misunderstandings. Showing his Australian English-speaking friend's post where internet slang is frequently used, he said:

> "On SNSs, internet slang or internet language is used a lot. So, I had a difficulty in understanding them. Yes, I strongly agree with it (the questionnaire)" (i27march18masaki).

At the same time, he stated:

> "It is a kind of English learning for me to get to know Internet slang" (i27march18masaki).

Although he was confronted with the difficulty of understanding internet slang, he still was motivated to learn it. Five out of the seven interviewees, Kei, Noriko, Go, Hiro, and Masaki, held positive attitudes towards English Internet slang, mentioning that it is part of the English language. Yuta did not comment about it negatively or positively, and only Suzu, who aimed to acquire 'perfect' English, showed her negative feelings towards Internet slang. This example shows the possibility that Internet slang in English functioned as an indicator for some

Chapter 12

participants to show themselves as fluent English users who have command of non-standard forms of the language.

Given the results above, it is interpreted that some interviewees constrained their Japanese identity through avoiding sharing their private information on SNSs. Some tried to construct their identity as fluent English speakers by learning Internet slang on SNSs.

4. Conclusions

SNSs are valuable tools for ELLs to practise their skills in an informal environment and to maintain and develop social connections with non-Japanese partners following a study abroad experience. The data revealed that participants changed their usage of SNSs over the course of their study abroad experience. Some notable changes included adoption of platforms not commonly used in Japan and adaptation to behaviours and norms of SNS usage in the target culture. Fear of flaunting one's English ability reduced usage of SNSs with one participant, but the effect of these barriers was reduced following study abroad. Finally, students participating in the study found that differences in cultural norms caused some tension in their interactions on SNS and forced them to negotiate their identity as they navigated these unfamiliar behaviours.

While every effort was made to strengthen the methodology used to collect data for this research, some limitations exist that must be considered. First, the data were collected from a small sample of students at one selective university. A larger, more diverse group of students would help to extrapolate the results to a larger population in Japan. In addition, a larger sample would allow for further quantitative analysis of the data collected. Second, the responses of the participants were self-reported. In order to address this issue in future studies, it will be important to triangulate the self-reported data by observing interactions on the platform. More accurate data regarding usage of SNSs might be gathered by having participants maintain a usage log.

Despite the limitations mentioned, the current study paints an interesting picture of several aspects important to the negotiation of identity in SNSs for ELLs in general, and Japan in particular. It is the hope of the researchers that this chapter will serve as a springboard for further research on the topic and help educators and administrators to better prepare study abroad participants to make the best use of SNSs before, during, and after their sojourn.

Acknowledgements

We would like to thank the Japan Society for the Promotion of Science who provided funding to two of the authors to conduct research on the topic of this chapter and share that research with the academic community.

References

Harrison, R., & Thomas, M. (2009). Identity in online communities: social networking sites and language learning. *International Journal of Emerging Technologies & Society*, 7(2), 109-124.

Ishii, K. (2017). A comparative study between Japanese, US. Taiwanese and Chinese social networking site users: self-disclosure and network homogeneity. In A. S. Telleria (Ed.), *Between the public and private in mobile communication* (pp. 154-175). Routledge.

Leis, A. (2014). Encouraging autonomy through the use of a social networking system. *The JALT CALL Journal*, 10(1), 69-80.

Lui, D., Kirschner, P. A., & Karpinski, A. C. (2017). A meta-analysis of the relationship of academic performance and social network site use among adolescents and young adults. *Computers in Human Behavior*, 77, 148-157. https://doi.org/10.1016/j.chb.2017.08.039

Norton, B. (2000). *Identity and language learning: gender, ethnicity and educational change.* Pearson Education Limited.

Ottoson, K. (2014). Study-abroad program assessment through social networking sites. *KOTESOL Proceedings 2014 Embracing Change: Blazing New Frontiers Through Language Teaching* (pp. 161-170).

Pavlenko, A., & Blackledge, A. (2004). Introduction: new theoretical approaches to the study of negotiation of identities in multilingual contexts. In A. Pavlenko & A. Blackledge (Eds), *Negotiation of identity in multilingual contexts* (pp. 1-33). Multilingual Matters Ltd. https://doi.org/10.21832/9781853596483-003

Pavlenko, A., & Norton, B. (2007). Identity, language learning and imagined communities. In J. Cummins & C. Davison (Eds), *International handbook of education: English language teaching* (Vol. 2) (pp. 669-680). Springer. https://doi.org/10.1007/978-0-387-46301-8_43

Sensis. (2017). Sensis social media report 2017. https://irp-cdn.multiscreensite.com/535ef142/files/uploaded/Sensis-Social-Media-Report-2017.pdf#search='sensis+socialmedia+report+2017'

Statista. (2018a). *Snapchat penetration rate in the Asia Pacific region in 2016, by region*. https://www.statista.com/statistics/858747/snapchat-penetration-rate-asia-and-the-pacific-by-region/

Statista. (2018b). Most popular social networks in Japan as of October 2017, ranked by audience reach. https://www.statista.com/statistics/258849/most-popular-social-networks-in-japan-ranked-by-reach/

Statista. (2018c). Japan: social network audience reach 2017. https://www.statista.com/statistics/258849/most-popular-social-networks-in-japan-ranked-by-reach/

Toland, S., Mills, D. J., & Kohyama, M. (2016). Enhancing Japanese university students' English-language presentation skills with mobile-video recordings. *JALT CALL Journal*, 12(3), 179-201.

Vasilopoulos, G. (2015). Language learner investment and identity negotiation in the Korean EFL context. *Journal of Language, Identity & Education*, 14(1), 61-79. https://doi.org/10.1080/15348458.2015.1019783

Waragai, I., Kurabayashi, S., Ohta, T., Raindl, M., Kiyoki, Y., & Tokuda, H. (2014). Context-aware writing support for SNS: connecting formal and informal learning. In S. Jager, L. Bradley, E. J. Meima & S. Thouësny (Eds), C*ALL Design: Principles and Practice - Proceedings of the 2014 EUROCALL Conference, Groningen, The Netherlands (*pp. 403-407). Research-publishing.net. https://doi.org/10.14705/rpnet.2014.000253

Author index

D
Dogan, Betul Eroglu 4, 87

F
Flores, Sandra 3, 39

G
Giannikas, Christina Nicole 1, 6, 145
Gorham, Tom 5, 101
Goria, Cecilia 4, 87

J
Jubaed, Sam 5, 101

K
Kakoulli Constantinou, Elis 1, 4, 55
Kilvinski, Bryan 4, 87
Kitano, Chika 6, 181
Kılıçkaya, Ferit 5, 131
Kohyama, Megumi 6, 181
Konstantinidis, Angelos 4, 87

L
Lopes, António 6, 159

M
Mills, Daniel J. 6, 181
Morales, Sandra 3, 39

N
Neokleous, Georgios 5, 117

P
Papadima-Sophocleous, Salomi 1, 3, 25

S
Sanyal, Tannishtha 5, 101
Soulé, María Victoria 3, 25
Starr, Emma L. 5, 101

T
Trajtemberg, Claudia 3, 39
Tseng, Jun-Jie 4, 71

W
Waldren, Sofía Milagros 3, 11

www.ingramcontent.com/pod-product-compliance
Lightning Source LLC
Chambersburg PA
CBHW022008160426
43197CB00007B/335